365 Stories and Rhymes for Boys

Every effort has been made to acknowledge the contributors to this book.
If we have made any errors, we will be pleased to rectify them in future editions.

This is a Parragon book
This edition published in 2006

Parragon
Queen Street
4 Queen Street
Bath BA1 1HE, UK

Design and project management by Aztec Design

Page make-up by
Mik Martin, Caroline Reeves, and Kilnwood Graphics

ISBN 1-40547-871-3
Printed in China

365 Stories and Rhymes for Boys

p

Contents

Little Hare; Round About; Ten o'Clock
   Scholar; The Giant; To the Magpie;
   John Smith   10
The Squirrel; Go to Bed, Tom; Charlie
   Warley; Daddy; Tom he Was
   a Piper's Son   11
The Naughty Bears   12
Round and Round the Garden;
   Teddy Bear, Teddy Bear;
   The Wheels on the Bus   18
Hey, Diddle, Diddle; Dingle Dangle

Scarecrow; If You're Happy
   and You Know It   19
The Bunny Olympics   20
Horse Power   22
Lost and Alone   26
Scrub Your Dirty Face; It's Raining,
   It's Pouring; One Finger, One
   Thumb; Rain, Rain, Go Away   28
Blow, Wind, Blow!; Sneeze on Monday;
   Clap Your Hands; Jackanory   29
There's No Room Here   30
The Great Egg Hunt   31
Wonky Bear   32
Willie Wastle; Ride Away; Bow-wow;
   Spin Dame; The Robin and the
   Wren; Parliament Soldiers   36
On Oath; Greedy Tom; Richard Dick;
   Bless You; Punctuality; A Rat;
   Diddlety, Diddlety; Milking   37
Naughty Chester Chick   38
The Chirpy Chatty Chicks   39
The Good Old Days   40
Way Down Yonder in the Maple
   Swamp; Old Roger is Dead; Follow
   My Bangalorey Man; See-saw,
   Sacradown   44
Over the Hills and Far Away; As I Was
   Going Along; A Sailor Went to Sea;
   From Wibbleton to Wobbleton   45
Leo Makes a Friend   46

The Magic Tree 48
Bobby's Best Birthday Present 52
Smelly Pup 56
A Spelling Lesson 58
Witch's Brew 59
The Three Jovial Welshmen;
    One, Two, Three, Four, Five;
    Five Little Monkeys 60
I Love Sixpence; One, Two, Buckle
    My Shoe; Three Young Rats 61
Birthday Bunnies 62
One Dark Night 68
Staying at Grandma's 70
Custard's New Home 74

Humpty Dumpty; We're All in the
    Dumps; Daffy-Down-Dilly;
    Tweedle-dum and Tweedle-dee 76
Cushy Cow Bonny; Hector Protector;
    Higglety, Pigglety, Pop!;
    There Was a Piper 77
Ducks for a Day 78
Monkey Mayhem 80
Lizzie and the Tractor 84
The Littlest Pig 86
Making a Splash! 90
Betty Pringle; If Wishes Were Horses;
    Jack be Nimble; As I Walked
    by Myself 92
Yankee Doodle; If All the World was
    Apple-pie; Fire on the Mountain;
    The Man in the Wilderness 93
Take the Ghost Train 94
Ode to Ghosts 95

Lazy Teddy 96
All at Sea 100
Benny the Barmy Builder 102
Tiger Tricks 106
This Little Piggy; To Market, to
    Market, to Buy a Fat Pig; To Market,
    To Market; Two Little Men in a
    Flying Saucer; Jim Crow 108
I Can…; Higgledy Piggledy; Tumbling;
    Two Fat Gentlemen; Lie a-Bed 109
Jack and the Beanstalk 110
Hide and Seek 116
Fred the Fearless Fireman 118
The Smiley Crocodile 122
Hark the Robbers; Handy Spandy,
    Jack-a-Dandy; There was a
    Crooked Man 124
My Father he Died; I Hear Thunder;
    Three Wise Men of Gotham 125

Who Can Save the Chicks?   126
It's Not Fair   127
Greedy Bear   128
The Chicklings   132
Hippo's Holiday   134
The Spooks' Ball   138
The Haunted House   139
I Saw a Slippery, Slithery Snake;
    Round About There; Foxy's Hole;
    Leg Over Leg; Head, Shoulders,
    Knees and Toes   140
Clap, Clap Hands; Shoes; Tommy Trot;
    Tall Shop; Five Little Soldiers   141
Hooray for Pepper   142
Buried Treasure   144
If You Hold My Hand   148
The Golden Bird   150
The Fluff Monsters   154
Once I Saw a Little Bird; Intery,
    Mintery, Cutery, Corn; Little Robin
    Redbreast; The North Wind
    Doth Blow   156

While We Were Walking; Two Little
    Dicky Birds; The Cuckoo; Little
    Wind; Magpies; Jay-bird   157
Crocodile Smiles   158
Desmond Grows Up   164
Mr Squirrel Won't Sleep   166
Danny Duckling in Trouble   170
Oh Dear, What Can the Matter Be?;
    Goosey Goosey Gander; Knick
    Knack Paddy Whack   172
Jack and Jill; Cock-a-Doodle-Doo;
    Girls and Boys Come Out to Play   173
Little Tim and his Brother Sam   174
Don't Care; Where Go the Boats?;
    The Oxen   178
Eldorado; The Mouse's Lullaby;
    The Duel   179
I Wish…   180

A Whale of a Time 181
Lost for Ever 182
Bone Crazy 186
Little Jack Jingle; Little Tommy
    Tittlemouse; Harry Parry; Young
    Roger Came Tapping; Jack, Jack,
    the Bread's a-Burning 188
Robin and Richard; If a Pig Wore a
    Wig; Tom, Tom, the Piper's Son;
    Jack and Guy; Bob Robin 189
Milly the Greedy Puppy 190
Tractor Trouble 192
The Smart Bear and the Foolish Bear 196
Pigs will be Pigs 198
Old Everest 202
Pop Goes the Weasel; Hot Cross
    Buns!; Oats and Beans; Pease
    Pudding Hot 204
Sing a Song of Sixpence; Five Little
    Peas; Five Fat Sausages; Robin
    the Bobbin 205
Little Dog Lost 206
One Bad Bunny 212
The Naughty Broom 214
The New Cat 218
Dance, Thumbkin, Dance; A Face
    Game; Clap Hands; Wash, Hands,
    Wash 220
Here's the Lady's Knives and Forks;
    Ten Little Fingers; My Hands; Row,
    Row, Row Your Boat 221
The Dotty Professor 222
My Funny Family 223
Bouncy Bunny 224
One Stormy Night 228
Good Teamwork 230
Monty the Mongrel 234
Loves to Sing!; Busy Farmer;
    Did You Know?; Where Are You? 236
Watch Out!; Back to the Farm; Kittens
    are Cuddly; Without a Growl 237
Bumble Bee Helps Out 238
The Yellow Digger 240
A Perfect Puppy 244
Birthday Bear 246
Chalk and Cheese 250
Alone; All the Bells Were Ringing; There
    Was an Old Man With a Beard 252
Hurt No Living Thing; Going
    Downhill on a Bicycle; Bread and
    Milk for Breakfast 253

Barney the Boastful Bear 254
Little Chick Lost 260
Snowy and Blowy 262
Easter Bunnies 266
Old Joe Brown; Poor Old Robinson
    Crusoe!; Old John Muddlecombe;
    Michael Finnegan 268
Tommy Thumb; Rub-a-dub Dub;
    Solomon Grundy; Jack Sprat 269
Clumsy Fred 270
Oscar the Octopus 271
Mr Mole Gets Lost 272
Not Another Bear 276
Yes You Can! 277
Bottoms Up! 278
Home Sweet Home 282
Moo! Moo! Moo!; You Need a Cow!;

Counting Sheep; Woolly Coats 284
Clip, Clop!; A Horse of Course!;
    Egg Hatching Dream; One Hen
    Pecking 285
Honey Bear and the Bees 286
A Scary Adventure 288
Where's Wanda? 292
The Mean King and the Crafty Lad 294
No One Like You 298
There Was a Man, and His Name
    Was Dob; Me, Myself, and I;
    Swan Swam Over the Sea; Hey,
    Dorolot, Dorolot! 300
My Grandmother Sent Me; Adam
    and Eve and Pinchme; Peter Piper;
    Robert Rowley 301
Peter Meets a Dragon 302
Sniffle 306
You Can Do It, Dilly Duck! 308
Tiger Tales 310
Chasing Tails 314
Hannah Bantry; Eeper Weeper;
    Go to Bed; Sippity, Sippity Sup; Where
    Am I?; Little Blue Ben;
    Dame Trot 316
I Do Not Like Thee; Sunshine;
    Old Bandy Legs; My Mummy's
    Maid; One, Two; One Little Indian;
    Charlie Wag 317
Bear Finds a Friend 318
Bears Picnic 319
The Sad Clown 320
Cheeky Chick 324

The Boy Who Wished Too Much 326

Ebby the Smallest Pup 330

The Grand Old Duke of York; What is
the Rhyme for Porringer?; Old King
Cole; Grey Goose and Gander 332

Ten Little Men; When Famed King
Arthur Ruled This Land; There
Was a King and he had Three
Daughters; The Queen of Hearts 333

Bunny Tails 334

Tabby Cat and the Cockerel 336

Fierce Tiger 340

The Invisible Imp 342

Polly Piglet's Surprise Party 346

Red Sky; Rain; Washing Up;
What's the News?; My Hobby
Horse; A Man in the Wilderness;
Robin Hood 348

Cobbler, Cobbler; There Was a Little
Boy; And That's All; The Little
Rusty, Dusty Miller; Warning;
Mr East's Feast 349

Rumpelstiltskin 350

Little Bunny and the Bully 356

Leap Frog 358

Sparky the Baby Dragon 362

Catch Him; Wine and Cakes;
Jack-a-Dandy; Punctuate; Marching;
Did You See My Wife?; Rain;
Tommy's Shop 364

King Boggen; Pit, Pat; Bagpipes;
Green Cheese; The Priest; Shrovetide;
Mother? 365

The Lost Lion 366

Simple Simon; Peter, Peter, Pumpkin
Eater; Johnny Shall Have a New
Bonnet; There Was a Little Boy 370

Wee Willie Winkie; Billy Booster;
Tommy Snooks and Bessy Brooks;
When Jacky's a Very Good Boy;
Little Tommy Tucker 371

Little Bunny 372

Little Bear 373

The Squeaky Van 374

A Goodnight Kiss 378

Night Sounds; In Dreams;
My Shadow 380

From a Railway Carriage; The Wind;
Spellbound; Good Night 381

Night-night Bear 382

Index 383

Little Hare

Round about there
  Sat a little hare,
The bow-wows came and chased him
  Right up there!

Round About

Round about the rose bush,
  Three steps,
Four steps,
  All the little boys and girls
Are sitting
  On the doorsteps.

Ten o'Clock Scholar

A diller, a dollar,
  A ten o'clock scholar,
What makes you come so soon?
  You used to come at ten o'clock,
But now you come at noon.

The Giant

Fee, fi, fo, fum,
  I smell the blood of
    an Englishman:
Be he alive or be he dead,
  I'll grind his bones
    to make my bread.

To the Magpie

Magpie, magpie, flutter and flee,
  Turn up your tail and good luck come to me.

John Smith

Is John Smith within?
  Yes, that he is.
Can he set a shoe?
  Aye, marry, two;
Here a nail and there a nail,
  Tick, tack, too.

10

The Squirrel

The winds they did blow,
   The leaves they did wag;
Along came a beggar boy,
   And put me in his bag.

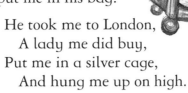

He took me to London,
   A lady me did buy,
Put me in a silver cage,
   And hung me up on high.

With apples by the fire,
   And nuts for me to crack,
Besides a little feather bed
   To rest my little back.

Go to Bed, Tom

Go to bed, Tom,
   Go to bed, Tom,
Tired or not, Tom,
   Go to bed, Tom.

Charlie Warley

Charley Warley had a cow,
   Black and white about the brow;
Open the gate and let her through,
   Charley Warley's old cow.

Daddy

Bring Daddy home
   With a fiddle and a drum,
A pocket full of spices,
   An apple and a plum.

Tom He Was a Piper's Son

Tom, he was a piper's son,
   He learnt to play when he was young,
And all the tune that he could play,
   Was, "Over the hills and far away".

Over the hills and a great way off,
   The wind shall blow my topknot off.

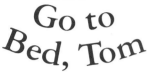

The Naughty Bears

One sunny summer's day, Ben and Fraser's parents told them to pack their things, as they were going to the beach.

"Yippee!" said Ben. "Can we take our teddies?"

"As long as you keep an eye on them this time," said Daddy. "We don't want to spend all afternoon looking everywhere for them if you lose them again!"

Ben and Fraser took their teddies everywhere they went, but they were always losing them, and then there was a great hunt to find them. But the truth was, that when no one was looking, the naughty little teddies would run away in search of excitement and adventure.

Today was no different. The family arrived at the beach and unpacked their things. Daddy sat reading a newspaper and Mummy took out a book. Soon Ben and Fraser were busy building sandcastles. When the naughty teddies saw that no one was looking, they jumped up and ran away giggling, all along the beach.

"Let's go exploring," said Billy, who was the oldest bear. "I can see a cave over there." He pointed to a dark hole in the rocks close to the water.

"It looks a bit dark and scary," said Bella.

"Don't be silly," said Billy. "You're a bear, aren't you? I thought that bears liked dark caves!"

The little bears clambered over the rocks and into the cave. It was very deep, and very dark. Just then, Bella spotted something gleaming on the floor. She picked it up and showed it to Billy.

"Gold!" said Billy, in excitement, taking the little coin from Bella. "This must be a smugglers' cave! Maybe the smugglers are still here. Let's take a look!"

"No!" said Bella. "They could be dangerous. Let's go back." She turned and ran back outside, where she saw to her horror that while they had been exploring the tide had come in, and cut the rocks off from the beach.

"Billy!" she called. "Come quickly, we're stranded!"

Meanwhile, Ben and Fraser had finished making sandcastles and found that their teddy bears were missing.

"Oh, no," groaned Daddy. "Not again!"

The family hunted high and low along the beach, but there was no sign of the bears to be found. "Maybe they've been washed out to sea," said Fraser, his voice trembling at the thought.

Back at the cave the naughty teddies could see their owners looking for them. They jumped up and down and waved their paws. "It's no use," said Bella, "they can't see us. We're too small."

"Don't worry," said Billy, trying to sound braver than he felt.

Just then, two men appeared from the other side of the rocks. The teddies froze – these must be the smugglers! They trembled in fear as the men picked them up, clambered over

the rocks, and tossed them into a little boat that had been hidden from view behind the rocks. The teddies clung together at the bottom of the boat as the men jumped in and began to row. Where were they taking them?

"Oh, Billy, I'm so frightened," whispered Bella. "Do you think they are going to hurt us?"

"No, Bella, I'm sure we'll be fine," answered Billy. But inside he didn't feel so sure. He was really very worried that they would never get home or see Ben and Fraser again.

Bella started to cry in little muffled whimpers, and big tears rolled down her cheeks. "If we ever get back home, I'm never going to run away again," she sobbed.

"There, there," comforted Billy, patting her gently.

After a while, the boat stopped and the men jumped out. They grabbed the bears and held them in the air high above their heads. One of the men called out in a loud voice, "Has anyone lost these bears?"

Everyone on the beach looked up, and Ben and Fraser raced over and grabbed their bears.

Daddy came running over to join them. He and the boys thanked the men for bringing the bears back. "We've been looking everywhere for them," said Ben and Fraser, grinning with relief.

"We found them up by that cave," said one of the men, pointing over to the cave. "You kids must have left them there."

"But the boys have been here building sandcastles all afternoon…" said Daddy, looking puzzled.

No one ever did find out how the naughty teddies got to the cave, or where the little coin in Billy's pocket came from. But from then on Daddy said they had to stay at home. The naughty teddies didn't really mind. They'd had enough adventures for the time being. And it gave them lots of time to play their favourite game – hide and seek!

Round and Round the Garden

Round and round the garden,
Like a teddy bear.
One step, two steps,
Tickly under there!

Round and round the haystack,
Went the little mouse.
One step, two steps,
In this little house.

Teddy Bear, Teddy Bear

Teddy bear, teddy bear,
Turn around.
Teddy bear, teddy bear,
Touch the ground.
Teddy bear, teddy bear,
Show your shoe.
Teddy bear, teddy bear,
That will do.
Teddy bear, teddy bear,
Go upstairs.
Teddy bear, teddy bear,
Say your prayers.
Teddy bear, teddy bear,
Turn out the light.
Teddy bear, teddy bear,
Say good night.

The Wheels on the Bus

The wheels on the bus go round and round,
Round and round, round and round,
The wheels on the bus go round and round,
All day long.

The wipers on the bus go swish, swish, swish,
Swish, swish, swish, swish, swish, swish,
The wipers on the bus go swish, swish, swish,
All day long.

The horn on the bus goes beep! beep! beep!
Beep! beep! beep! beep! beep! beep!
The horn on the bus goes beep! beep! beep!
All day long.

The people on the bus go chat, chat, chat,
Chat, chat, chat, chat, chat, chat,
The people on the bus go chat, chat, chat,
All day long.

The children on the bus bump up and down,
Up and down, up and down,
The children on the bus bump up and down,
All day long.

Hey, Diddle, Diddle

Hey, diddle, diddle, the cat and the fiddle,
The cow jumped over the moon;
The little dog laughed to see such sport,
And the dish ran away with the spoon!

Dingle Dangle Scarecrow

When all the cows were sleeping
And the sun had gone to bed,
Up jumped the scarecrow
And this is what he said:

I'm a dingle dangle scarecrow
With a flippy floppy hat!
I can shake my arms like this,
I can shake my legs like that!

When the cows were in the meadow
And the pigeons in the loft,
Up jumped the scarecrow
And whispered very soft:
Chorus

When all the hens were roosting
And the moon behind a cloud,
Up jumped the scarecrow
And shouted very loud:
Chorus

If You're Happy and You Know It

If you're happy and you know it,
Clap your hands.
If you're happy and you know it,
Clap your hands.
If you're happy and you know it,
And you really want to show it,
If you're happy and you know it,
Clap your hands.

If you're happy and you know it,
Nod your head, etc.

If you're happy and you know it,
Stamp your feet, etc.

If you're happy and you know it,
Say "ha, ha!", etc.

If you're happy and you know it,
Do all four!

The Bunny Olympics

Everyone on Fiddlestick Farm was really excited – today was the Bunny Olympics. Rabbits hopped and skipped from all around, to find out who would be the champion runner, jumper and muncher!

All the animals helped to get things ready. Goat and Pig put out the plant pots for the Hopping-In-and-Out Race. Then, it was time to start... READY, STEADY, GO!

BOING! BOING! BOING! Up and down and in and out of the plant pots went those bunnies, as fast as they could go! Charlie won easily, but then had to go back and rescue his little sister Bubbles, who was stuck inside the very first pot!

Next, it was time for the High Jump. Cow and Horse held the rope, while the bouncy bunnies jumped higher and higher until... WHEEEEEE! Ellie Bunny leapt right over Horse's back!

"No one will be able to jump higher than that!" mooed Cow. "Ellie wins the High Jump!"

Down in the meadow, near the stream, rabbits were competing in the Long Jump competition. Suddenly – SPLOOSH! Freddie Bunny leapt so far, he landed straight in the water! No one

else could jump that far, so Freddie Bunny was the winner!

The Munching Contest was next. Sheep was in charge of counting how many carrots and lettuces had been eaten.

Patty Bunny munched eight carrots. Little Bobo ate three lettuces and Nicky Bunny chomped through ten carrots and five lettuces.

Then – "BUUUUURP!" burped Harry, the biggest bunny, very loudly. "Pardon me," he said.

"Goodness!" said Sheep, in surprise. "Why, Harry, you've managed to gobble twenty carrots and ten whole lettuces! You are our Champion Muncher!"

Finally, it was time for the Obstacle Race. All the rabbits lined up at the starting line. How the farm animals cheered, as the bunnies hopped, bounced and skipped over the stream, except little Bubbles, who wanted to stay and paddle! Then, Harry got stuck when he tried to bounce through the hollow log and everyone had to push him through! They squeezed under the strawberry nets, hopped over the bales of hay and, huffing and puffing, dashed back to the old tractor and past the finishing line. But who was the winner?

They all were! Every one of the bunnies had crossed the finishing line together, so they all shared the first prize – a great, big, juicy carrot! And, as the sun began to set, everyone agreed it had been a great Bunny Olympics!

Horse Power

On the day of the County Show, there was hustling and bustling on the farm. Mrs MacDonald had to feed the animals and collect the eggs by herself, because Old MacDonald was busy cleaning his tractor.

Every year, Old MacDonald gave rides on his tractor and trailer to the children. They loved it, but it was a lot of hard work for the farmer, with wheels to wash, and paintwork to polish. Today, he also had ducks to shoo away when they began splashing about in the bubbles in his bucket!

But, at last, the tractor was spotlessly clean. Old MacDonald went into the farmhouse to put on his best boots.

"Here we go," said Doris the duck, as the farmer climbed into his tractor. "Cover your ears, little ones!"

But, when Old MacDonald turned the key, there was silence. The tractor simply would not start.

Old MacDonald tweaked the engine – and got his hands greasy. He stamped and stomped around – and got his best boots muddy. He muttered and moaned – and got rather red in the face. None of it did any good. The tractor didn't cough or splutter or show any sign of life.

"I hate to let the children down," groaned Old MacDonald. "But I can't pull the trailer if I don't have a tractor."

Now, Henry the cockerel is naughty and nosy, but sometimes he has good ideas. Henry jumped up on to Old George and Tilly's stable door and gave his loudest, "Cock-a-doodle-doo!"

Old MacDonald looked up in surprise, and then he gave a big smile.

"Goodness, gracious me!" he cried. "You're right, Henry – horse power! Now quick, jump out of the way. There's lots of work to be done!"

There were tails to untangle, coats to comb, and manes to thread with ribbons. There were harnesses to hitch and reins to clean and hang with gleaming brasses.

"It's just like the good old days," neighed Old George to Tilly.

There was no doubt who the stars of the County Show were that year. Children queued for ages, waiting to be pulled around by Old George and Tilly, who plodded proudly up and down with their coats shining and their heads held high.

At the end of the afternoon, Old MacDonald led the horses home and gave them a special supper of apples and oats.

"You know," he said with a sigh as he stroked their manes, "I miss the old days, too."

Old George and Tilly nodded their great heads, but it wasn't to show they agreed with him. They were asleep on their feet – they're not as young as they used to be, and it had been a very busy day!

Lost and Alone

Deep in the jungle, Mungo was trying to slip off through the trees. "Mungo, tell me where you're going, please," called Mum. "What are you planning to do today?"

"I'm just going to play," smiled Mungo.

"Okay," said Mum. "But no monkey business!"

Elephant was enjoying a drink, when Mungo crept up and yelled, "Hi, Elephant! Want to play?" Then he added, "I know a good game."

"Oh, yes?" said Elephant, suspiciously. "What's its name?"

"Funny faces!" said Mungo. "What do you say?"

"I'm not sure," said Elephant. "I don't know how to play."

"Easy," said Mungo. "All you have to do, is pull a funny face. Look, I'll show you." And he took hold of Elephant's trunk. Mungo wound Elephant's trunk round and slipped the end through. He pulled it into a knot. "Wow, Elephant!" he giggled. "What a funny face you've got!"

"Hey!" gurgled Elephant. "How do I get out of this?" But Mungo was gone!

Lion was trying to have a laze in the sun, when Mungo swung down and asked, "Want some fun?" Then he added, "Come on. I know a good game."

"Yeah?" said Lion, suspiciously. "What's its name?"

"Funny faces," said Mungo. "What do you say?"

"I'm not sure," said Lion. "I don't know how to play."

"Easy," said Mungo. "All you have to do, is pull a funny face. Look, I'll show you." And he took hold of Lion's bottom lip. Mungo pulled the lip up over Lion's nose. "You see," he said, "that's the way it goes."

Then he ran off, smiling, through the trees. "Forget what Mum said," thought Mungo. "I'll do as I please." He swung through the branches, but, after a while, Mungo's face lost its smile. "I don't know where I am!" he wailed.

"That's a funny face," said Elephant. "He wins the game for sure."

"It's not a game," howled Mungo. "I'm lost and alone. I want my mum! How do I get out of here? This isn't any fun!"

"Well, shall we help him?" Lion roared. "What do you think?"

"I'm not sure," said Elephant. "He did disturb my drink."

"He wrecked my rest, too," Lion said. "You're not the only one."

"If we agree to help, Mungo," the animals said, "then no more funny faces. Can you get that into your head?"

Mungo looked much happier than he'd done in quite a while. "No more tricks!" Mungo promised, and he thanked both of them. "Being lost and alone wasn't any fun for me!"

Scrub Your Dirty Face

Scrub your dirty face,
  Scrub your dirty face,
With a rub-a-dub-dub,
  And a rub-a-dub-dub,
Scrub your dirty face.

It's Raining, It's Pouring

It's raining, it's pouring,
  The old man is snoring;
He went to bed and bumped his head
  And couldn't get up in the morning.

One Finger, One Thumb

One finger, one thumb, keep moving,
  One finger, one thumb, keep moving,
One finger, one thumb, keep moving,
  We'll all be merry and bright.

One finger, one thumb, one arm, keep moving,
  One finger, one thumb, one arm, keep moving,
One finger, one thumb, one arm, keep moving,
  We'll all be merry and bright.

Rain, Rain, Go Away

Rain, rain,
  Go away,
Come again
  Another day.

One finger, one thumb, one arm, one leg, keep moving,
  One finger, one thumb, one arm, one leg, keep moving,
One finger, one thumb, one arm, one leg, keep moving,
  We'll all be merry and bright.

One finger, one thumb, one arm, one leg,
  one nod of the head, keep moving,
One finger, one thumb, one arm, one leg,
  one nod of the head, keep moving,
One finger, one thumb, one arm, one leg,
  one nod of the head, keep moving,
We'll all be merry and bright.

Blow, Wind, Blow!

Blow, wind, blow! and go, mill, go!
  That the miller may grind his corn;
That the baker may take it,
  And into rolls make it,
And send us some hot in the morn.

Sneeze on Monday

Sneeze on Monday, sneeze for danger;
  Sneeze on Tuesday, kiss a stranger;
Sneeze on Wednesday, get a letter;
  Sneeze on Thursday, something better;
Sneeze on Friday, sneeze for sorrow;
  Sneeze on Saturday, see your sweetheart tomorrow.

Clap Your Hands

Clap your hands, clap your hands,
  Clap them just like me.
Touch your shoulders, touch your shoulders,
  Touch them just like me.
Tap your knees, tap your knees,
  Tap them just like me.
Shake your head, shake your head,
  Shake it just like me.
Clap your hands, clap your hands,
  Then let them quiet be.

Jackanory

I'll tell you a story
  Of Jackanory,
And now my story's begun;
  I'll tell you another
Of Jack his brother,
  And now my story's done.

There's No Room Here!

It was a very hot day down on Apple Tree Farm. The chicks trotted off to sit in the cool barn – but the cows had got there first!

"There's no room in here for you chicks!" mooed Mrs Cow. "Try the duck pond." But the duck pond was full of splashing ducks!

"This is not a chick pond!" quacked Mrs Duck. So, the chicks waddled past the pigsty, where Mr Pig was rolling in a big, squidgy mudbath.

"That looks very cool," called the chicks, peeping round the fence.

"Yes!" grunted the greedy pig. "And it's all for me!"

Suddenly, Robbie Chick had an idea. "Come on!" he cried. "Follow me!" The three hot chicks followed him into the farmer's garden and, just at that moment, a fountain of water shot up in the air and splashed all the chicks! "Oooh! That's freezing!" giggled Rosie. "It feels great!"

The little chicks ran in and out of the cool water all afternoon, splashing and splishing about, until it was time for tea. On the way home, they saw that the sun had dried up Mr Pig's mudbath. The dippy ducks had splashed all the water out of the pond, and the cows had been taken for milking and were moaning in the hot milking parlour.

But the very cool chicks just chuckled and dripped their way back home to Mummy.

The Great Egg Hunt

On Sunnybrook Farm, there lived a very forgetful hen called Hetty. One day, Hetty laid a lovely clutch of five eggs, but then she couldn't remember where they were. She searched the farmyard. "Oh, where did I put my babies?" she cried. "I'm such a feather-brain!"

Dolly the duck rushed over to help. "Don't worry," quacked Dolly, kindly. "We'll soon find them." And she waddled off to get the other farm animals – the Great Egg Hunt had begun!

Jake the sheep found one of the eggs amongst the brambles! Gus the goat found another egg on top of an old cabbage leaf in the compost heap! Harry the horse found missing egg number three in a rabbit hole! Claudia the cow found egg number four in a cosy clump of hay!

"But there's still one missing! I laid five eggs!" squawked Hetty. Then, Penny the pig spotted something nestling under a very old wheelbarrow.

"Panic over," she oinked. "I've found it!"

"Hooray!" the other animals quacked, barked, neighed and mooed in delight. Sam the sheepdog scooped all the eggs on to an old sack and carried them back to the hen house. And so ended the Great Egg Hunt!

Hetty the hen was overjoyed! "Oh, thank you, thank you!" she clucked and quickly settled herself on top of the five eggs.

The next morning, one by one, five, fat, fluffy chicks hatched out! Hetty proudly took the baby chicks out of the hen house, to show the other farm animals.

Wonky Bear

Mr and Mrs Puppety owned an old-fashioned toy shop. They made toys by hand in a room at the back of the shop. But they were getting old and their eyesight was bad.

"It's time we got an apprentice toymaker," said Mr Puppety to his wife. They soon found a young lad called Tom to work for them. He worked hard and carefully. He spent his first week making a teddy bear. When he had finished he showed the bear to Mr and Mrs Puppety.

"He looks very cuddly," said Mrs Puppety.

Tom was pleased that they liked his bear and he went off home whistling happily.

"He really is a lovely bear," said Mr Puppety, "but his head is a bit wonky."

"I know," said his wife, "but it's Tom's first try. Let's just put him up there on the shelf with the other teddy bears."

That night Wonky Bear sat on the shelf and started to cry. He had heard what Mr and Mrs Puppety had said about him.

"What's wrong?" asked Brown Bear, who was sitting next to him.

"My head is on wonky," sobbed Wonky Bear.

"Does it hurt?" asked Brown Bear.

"No," replied Wonky Bear.

"Well then, why are you crying?" asked Brown Bear.

"Because nobody will want to buy a wonky bear. I'll be left in this shop forever and nobody will ever take me home and love me," he cried.

"Don't worry," said Brown Bear. "We've all got our faults, and you look fine to me. Just try your best to look cute and cuddly and you'll soon have someone to love you." This made Wonky Bear feel much happier and he fell fast asleep.

The next day the shop was full of people, but nobody paid any attention to Wonky Bear. Then a little boy looked up at the shelf and cried, "Oh, what a lovely bear. Can I have that one, Daddy?"

Wonky Bear's heart lifted as the little boy's daddy reached up to his shelf. But he picked up Brown Bear instead and handed him to the little boy. Wonky Bear felt sadder than ever. Nobody wanted him. All of his new friends would get sold and leave the shop, but he would be left on the shelf gathering dust. Poor old Wonky Bear!

Now, Mr and Mrs Puppety had a little granddaughter called Jessie who loved to visit the shop and play with the toys. All the toys loved her because she was gentle and kind. It so happened that the next time she came to visit it was her birthday, and her grandparents told her she could choose any toy she wanted as her present.

"I know she won't choose me," thought Wonky Bear sadly. "Not with all these other beautiful toys to choose from."

But, to Wonky's amazement, Jessie looked up and pointed at his shelf and said, "I'd like that wonky bear please. No one else will have a bear quite like him."

Mr Puppety smiled and gave Wonky to Jessie. She hugged and kissed him, and Wonky felt so happy he almost cried. She took him home and put a smart red bow around his neck ready for her birthday party.

He felt very proud indeed.

Soon the other children arrived, each carrying their teddy bears under their arms.

Wonky Bear could not believe his eyes when he saw the little boy with his friend Brown Bear!

"I'm having a teddy bears' picnic," Jessie explained to him, hugging him tight. All of the children and the bears had a wonderful time, especially Wonky. He had found a lovely home, met his old friend and made lots of new ones.

"See, I told you not to worry," said Brown Bear.

"I know," said Wonky. "And I never will again."

Willie Wastle

I, Willie Wastle,
  Stand on my castle,
An' a' the dogs o' your toon,
  Will no' drive Willie Wastle down.

Bow-wow

Bow-wow, says the dog,
  Mew, mew, says the cat,
Grunt, grunt, goes the hog,
  And squeak goes the rat.
Tu-whu, says the owl,
  Caw, caw, says the crow,
Quack, quack, says the duck,
  And what cuckoos say you know.

Ride Away

Ride away, ride away,
  Johnny shall ride,
He shall have a pussycat
  Tied to one side;
He shall have a little dog
  Tied to the other,
And Johnny shall ride
  To see his grandmother.

Spin Dame

Spin, Dame, spin,
  Your bread you must win;
Twist the thread and break it not,
  Spin, Dame, spin.

The Robin and the Wren

The robin and the wren,
  They fought upon the porridge pan;
But before the robin got a spoon,
  The wren had eaten the porridge down.

Parliament Soldiers

High diddle ding, did you hear the bells ring?
  The parliament soldiers are gone to the king.
Some they did laugh, and some they did cry,
  To see the parliament soldiers go by.

On Oath

As I went to Bonner,
  I met a pig
Without a wig,
  Upon my word and honour.

Richard Dick

Richard Dick upon a stick,
  Sampson on a sow,
We'll ride away to Colley fair
  To buy a horse to plough.

Punctuality

Be always in time,
  Too late is a crime.

Diddlety, Diddlety

Diddlety, diddlety, dumpty,
The cat ran up the plum tree;
Half a crown to fetch her down,
Diddlety, diddlety, dumpty.

Greedy Tom

Jimmy the Mowdy
  Made a great crowdy;
Barney O'Neal
  Found all the meal;
Old Jack Rutter
  Sent two stone of butter;
The Laird of the Hot
  Boiled it in his pot;
And Big Tom of the Hall
  He supped it all.

Bless You

Bless you, bless you, burnie-bee,
  Tell me when my wedding be;
If it be tomorrow day,
  Take your wings and fly away.
Fly to the east, fly to the west,
  Fly to him I love the best.

A Rat

There was a rat,
  for want of stairs,
Went down a rope
  to say his prayers.

Milking

Cushy cow, bonny, let down thy milk,
  And I will give thee a gown of silk;
A gown of silk and a silver tee,
  If thou wilt let down thy milk for me.

Naughty Chester Chick

Chester was a naughty chick,
    He really was quite bad
And every day, the things he did
    Would make his mum go mad!

He'd yell, "Ooh, quickly, Mary-Lou,
    There's something you should see!"
But while his sister took a look,
    He'd gobble up her tea!

He'd climb up on the hen house roof
    And crow just like his dad,
But Chester's screechy-scratchy yells
    Just drove the whole farm mad!

He'd wait until his poor, old mum
    Had settled for a nap
And then he'd run and, with a jump,
    He'd land right in her lap!

"All right! That's it! I've had enough!"
    His angry mummy cried.
"The others all can have a treat,
    But you must stay inside!"

So, Chester missed out on
        the treat,
    Which really was so sad,
Because they all had
        sunflower seeds,
    "My favourites!" moaned the lad.

"Mum, from now on,
        I'll be good!
    I promise!" Chester cried.
"I'm sorry I have been so bad.
    Please may I come outside?"

"All right," his mum said,
        "out you come!
    But, Chester, don't forget,
I don't give treats to naughty boys!"
    So, was Chester good? You bet!

The Chirpy Chatty Chicks

The mighty bull
    stomps from his stall.
  His great, big face peers
    round the wall.
But, just as he begins to shout,
  Five fluffy chicks come
    trotting out
And run around
  big Billy's feet.
    "Oh!" Billy cries.
    "You're really sweet!"

Poor Billy Bull can't get to sleep!
  Those chicks keep chirping, "Cheep!
    Cheep! Cheep!"
Each time he shuts his weary eyes,
  They wake him up with their
    loud cries.
"We're hungry, Mum!" they shout
  and yell.
  "Our tums are empty! Can't you tell?"

So, Billy Bull gets really mad.
  "I've had enough! I'll tell their Dad!
All day long, they chirp and cheep.
    I wouldn't mind – but
      I can't sleep!
        I'll never get to rest
      my head
      Until these noisy
  chicks are fed!"

So now the chicks have a new mate,
  Who thinks that they
    are really great
And doesn't mind that
  he can't sleep,
  Because they always cry,
    "Cheep! Cheep!"
He smiles now when they
  call to say,
  "Hey Billy! Please come
    out to play!"

The Good Old Days

On cold, wet and windy afternoons, when Old MacDonald lets his animals shelter in the warm barn, they like listening to stories. But, it does depend on who's telling the story!

The pigs tell tales about food. The hens' stories usually concern the ducks, and the cows are terrible gossips – they repeat things they have half-heard over the hedge!

But Old George and Tilly, the oldest animals on the farm, always talk about how much better it was in days gone by. This bores the other animals. They have heard them many times before.

One very cold spring day the farm was full of newborn chicks.

Old MacDonald went to the hen house and told Henrietta, "Take your babies into the barn. It will be much cosier there than in here."

"Baaa!" bleated Maria the sheep, who was standing near the barn door. "Did you hear that? Henrietta is bringing her chicks in. There'll be no peace now!"

Suddenly, there was mooing, neighing, snorting and quacking as the other animals all agreed. Those tiny chicks were the most troublesome little creatures on the farm. And the animals all stared in dismay as, one by one, the chicks filed in.

It was Percy the pig's turn to tell a story. "Once upon a time," he began, "there lived a pig who was very hungry..."

Although the animals tried to concentrate, the lively little chicks made it difficult to listen. They pecked at Heather the cow's nose, making her sneeze. They scratched at Bruce the sheepdog's tail until he was forced to bark quite sharply at them. One chick even tried to go to sleep in Maria the sheep's woolly ear. It was very distracting and it made all the animals cross.

"… something very, very delicious. The end," said Percy, aware that no one had been able to listen to his story. He oinked loudly at the chicks and stomped off into a corner to sulk.

Next, it was Old George the horse's turn. "My tale," he said, "is about the good old days…"

All the animals, except Tilly, groaned quietly. A boring story and a barn full of troublesome chicks was a recipe for a dreadfully dull afternoon.

However, as Old George droned on and on and on, an amazing thing happened. Each and every chirping chick began to fall asleep snug in the warmth of Henrietta's feathers.

"… and that reminds me of another story," said Old George, "but I don't expect you want to hear that today."

"Oh, yes! Yes, we do!" chorused the other animals. "We love your stories, George!" And this time they meant every word of it!

Way Down Yonder in the Maple Swamp

Way down yonder in the maple swamp
  The wild geese gather and the ganders honk;
The mares kick up and the ponies prance;
  The old sow whistles and the little pigs dance.

Old Roger is Dead

Old Roger is dead and
  gone to his grave,
H'm ha! gone to his grave.

They planted an apple tree
  over his head,
H'm ha! over his head.

The apples were ripe
  and ready to fall,
H'm ha! ready to fall.

There came an old woman
  and picked them all up,
H'm ha! picked them all up.

Old Roger jumped up and
  gave her a knock,
H'm ha! gave her a knock.

Which made the old woman
  go hippity hop,
H'm ha! hippity hop!

Follow My Bangalorey Man

Follow my Bangalorey Man,
  Follow my Bangalorey Man;
I'll do all that ever I can
  To follow my Bangalorey Man.
We'll borrow a horse, and steal a gig,
  And round the world we'll do a jig,
And I'll do all that ever I can
  To follow my Bangalorey Man!

See-saw, Sacradown

See-saw, Sacradown,
  Which is the way to London Town?
One foot up and one foot down,
  That's the way to London Town.

Over the Hills and Far Away

When I was young and had no sense
  I bought a fiddle for eighteen pence,
And the only tune that I could play
  Was "Over the Hills and Far Away".

As I Was Going Along

As I was going along, long, long,
  A-singing a comical song, song, song,
The lane that I went was so long, long, long,
  And the song that I sung was as long, long, long,
And so I went singing along.

A Sailor Went to Sea

A sailor went to sea, sea, sea,
  To see what he could see, see, see,
But all that he could see, see, see,
  Was the bottom of the deep blue sea, sea, sea.

From Wibbleton to Wobbleton

From Wibbleton to Wobbleton is fifteen miles,
  From Wobbleton to Wibbleton is fifteen miles,
From Wibbleton to Wobbleton,
  From Wobbleton to Wibbleton,
From Wibbleton to Wobbleton is fifteen miles.

Leo Makes a Friend

Leo was quite a shy lion. His mum and dad and brothers and sisters were all much bolder. Sometimes he was sad because he didn't have any friends.

"Mum," he said one day, "why will no one play with me?"

"They think you're frightening because you're a lion," said Mum.

It was a lovely day. Leo felt sure he would make a new friend today. He came to some trees where a group of small monkeys were playing. When the monkeys saw Leo they scampered to the top of the tallest trees.

"Hello," called out Leo. There was no answer. "Hello," he called again. "Won't you come down and play with me?"

There was silence. Then one of the monkeys blew a loud raspberry.

"Go away," he said rudely, "we don't like lions! Your teeth are too big," said the monkey, and giggled noisily.

Leo walked on until he came to a deep pool where a hippopotamus and her baby were bathing. Leo watched them playing in the water.

"Hi!" called out Leo. "Can I come in the water with you? I'd like to play," said Leo.

"So would I!" said Baby Hippo.

"No, you wouldn't," said Mummy Hippo firmly. "You don't play with lions."

Puzzled, Leo walked on. He came to an ostrich with its head buried in the sand. "What are you doing?" asked Leo in surprise.

"Hiding from you!" said the ostrich gruffly.

"But I can still see you!" said Leo.

"But I can't see you!" said the ostrich.

"Come and play with me instead," said Leo.

"Not likely," said the ostrich. "I don't play with lions, they roar!"

Leo walked on. He saw a snake sunbathing on a rock. He touched the snake gently with his paw. "Play with me," he said.

"Ouch!" said the snake. "Your claws are too sharp."

"I shall just have to get used to playing by myself," he thought.

Suddenly, he heard a small voice say, "Hello!"

Leo looked round. He could see a pair of yellow eyes peeping at him from behind a tree. "You won't want to play with me," said Leo grumpily, "I've got a loud roar, and sharp claws, *and* big teeth!"

"So have I," said the voice.

"What are you?" asked Leo, interested now.

"I'm a lion, of course!"

And into the clearing walked another little lion.

"I'm a lion, too," said Leo, grinning. "Would you like to share my picnic?"

"Yes, please!" said the other lion. They ate the picnic and played for the rest of the afternoon.

"I like being a lion," said Leo happily. He had made a friend at last!

The Magic Tree

Tommy rubbed his eyes, blinked hard, and looked out of his bedroom window again. But it was still there – an enormous oak tree that definitely hadn't been there yesterday! If it had been there, he'd have known all about it for sure. For a start he would have climbed up it, for Tommy loved nothing better than climbing trees.

No, this tree was definitely not there yesterday! Tommy sat staring at the tree in wonder and disbelief. The tree stood there, outside his bedroom window, with its huge, spreading branches almost asking to be climbed. Tommy wondered how on earth it had suddenly got there, but he decided that, before he wondered about that too much, he had better go and climb it first. After all, there was always time later to wonder about things but never enough time to do things, he thought.

As soon as he was dressed, he ran outside to take a closer look at the new tree. It seemed just like any other big oak tree. It had lots of wide, inviting branches and lots of green, rounded leaves. And it had deep, furrowed bark just like any other oak tree.

Tommy couldn't resist any longer – he began to climb. In no time at all, he was in a green, leafy canopy. He couldn't see the ground any more, but something was not quite right. The branches beneath his feet seemed to be so big that he could stand up on them and walk in any direction. And the branches around him were just like trees themselves. In fact, he suddenly realised that he wasn't climbing a tree any longer, but standing in a whole forest full of trees.

Tommy thought he had better get down. But where was down? All he could see were tall, swaying trees with twisty paths leading off even deeper into the forest. Tommy didn't know how he had done it, but he had got himself lost in a forest, and he hadn't even had breakfast yet!

Worse still, it seemed to be getting dark. "Quick, over here!" a voice suddenly called out. Tommy was very startled, but he was even more startled when he saw that the voice belonged to a squirrel.

"You can speak!" blurted out Tommy.

"Of course I can speak!" snapped the squirrel. "Now listen. You are in great danger, and there's no time to lose if we are to save you from the clutches of the evil Wizard of the Woods."

The squirrel quickly explained that, long ago, a spell had been cast on the forest and it had become enchanted. Every now and again, the

Wizard of the Woods lured an unsuspecting person into his realm by making a tree appear. Once you climbed the tree, you entered the forest. Escape was almost impossible.

"But why does the Wizard of the Woods want to lure people into the forest?" asked Tommy, knowing that he wouldn't like the answer.

"To turn them into fertiliser to make the trees grow," said the squirrel.

Tommy didn't really know what fertiliser was, but it sounded nasty. He was pleased when the squirrel suddenly said, "There is just one way to get you out of here. But we must hurry. Soon it will be dark and the Wizard of the Woods will awake. Once he awakes, he will smell your blood and he will capture you."

Jumping up the nearest tree, the squirrel called, "Follow me."

Tommy immediately climbed after the squirrel. "Where are we going?" he panted as they climbed higher and higher.

"To the top of the tallest tree in the forest," the squirrel answered as they clambered from tree to tree, climbing ever higher. "It's the only way to escape. You'll see!" said the squirrel.

Eventually they stopped climbing. Below them and around them was nothing but more trees. Tommy looked up, and at last he could see the clear, twilight sky. He also noticed something rather strange. All the leaves at the top of the tallest tree were enormous.

"Quick, time is running out," said the squirrel. "Sit on this leaf and hold tight."

Tommy sat on one of the huge leaves. The squirrel whistled, and before Tommy could blink he had been joined by a hundred more squirrels. They each took hold of the branch to which the leaf was attached. With a great heave, they pulled and pulled until the branch was bent backwards. Suddenly they let go. With a mighty "TWANG", the branch, with Tommy and the leaf attached, sprang forward. As it did so Tommy and the leaf were launched into the air. High above the trees they soared until, ever so slowly, they began to float down to earth. Down, down, they went, until they landed with a bump.

Tommy opened his eyes to find himself on his bedroom floor. He ran over to the window and looked out. The magic tree was nowhere to be seen. It had gone as quickly as it had appeared – perhaps it had never been there at all. Perhaps it had just been a dream... What do you think?

Bobby's Best Birthday Present

It was the morning of Bobby's birthday and he was very excited. When he came down to breakfast, there on the table was a big pile of presents. Bobby opened them one by one. There was a beautiful book with pictures of wild animals, a toy racing car and a baseball cap. Bobby was very pleased with his presents, but where was the present from his parents? "Close your eyes and hold out your hands!" said his mother. When he opened his eyes there was a large rectangular parcel in his hands. Bobby tore off the wrapping and inside was a box. And inside the box was a wonderful, shiny, electric train set.

For a moment, Bobby looked at the train set lying in the box. It was so lovely he could hardly bear to touch it. There was an engine and six carriages all lying neatly on their sides. Bobby carefully lifted the engine

out of the box. Then he set up the track and soon he had the train whizzing round his bedroom floor. Freddie the cat came in and watched the train going round. Round and round he watched it go, then one time when the train came past Freddie swiped at it with his paw and derailed it. The engine and the six carriages came tumbling off the track and landed in a heap on the floor. "Look what you've done!" wailed Bobby as he picked up the train and reassembled it. The carriages were undamaged, but the engine had hit the side of his bed and was really badly dented.

Bobby was very upset. "My brand new train is ruined!" he cried.

"Don't worry, Bobby," said his mother. "We can't take it back to the shop now, but we can take it to the toymender in the morning. I'm sure he'll make a good job of mending the engine and it'll look as good as new again." Bobby played with his racing car, he wore his new baseball cap and he read his new book, but really all he wanted to do was to play with his train set. He went to bed that night with the engine on the floor near his bed.

In the morning when Bobby woke up, the first thing he did was to look at the poor broken engine of his train set. He picked it up, expecting to see the buckled metal, but the engine was perfect. He couldn't believe his eyes! He ran to his parents. "Look, look!" he cried. They were as amazed as he was. The engine worked perfectly and Bobby played happily with his train set all day – but he made sure Freddie kept out of his room!

That night Bobby couldn't sleep. He lay in bed tossing and turning. Then he heard a noise. It was the sound of his train set rushing round the track. He peered into the darkness and, yes, he could definitely make out the shape of the train as it sped by. How had the train started? It couldn't start all by itself! Had Freddie crept into his room and flicked the switch? As his eyes gradually became accustomed to the dark Bobby

could make out shapes in the carriages. Who were the mysterious passengers? He slid out of bed and on to the floor beside the train set. Now he could see that the passengers were little folk wearing strange pointed hats and leafy costumes. "Elves!" thought Bobby.

At that moment one of the elves spotted Bobby. "Hello there!" he called as the train rushed past again. "We saw that your train set was broken. We so much wanted a ride that we fixed it. I hope you don't mind!" Bobby was too astounded to say anything at all. "Come with us for a ride," called the elf as his carriage approached again.

As the train passed him the elf leaned out of the carriage and grabbed Bobby by the hand. Bobby felt himself shrinking as he flew through the air, and the next instant he was sitting beside the elf in the carriage of his very own train set!

"Here we go – hold tight!" called the elf as the train left the track and went out through the window into the night sky.

"Now, where would you like to go? What would you like to see?" asked the elf.

"Toyland!" replied Bobby without hesitation. Sure enough, the train headed towards a track which curved up a mountain made of pink and white sugar.

Beside the track were toys going about their daily business. Bobby saw a ragdoll getting into a shiny tin car, then a wooden sailor puppet wound up the car with a large key and off went the doll. He saw three teddy bears setting off for school with their satchels on their backs.

The train stopped and Bobby and the elves got out. "Now for some fun!" said one of the elves. They had come to a halt by a toy fairground. Bobby found that this was like no other fairground he had ever been to before. For in Toyland, all the rides are real. The horses on the carousel were real horses. The Dodgem cars were real cars. And, when he got in the rocket for the rocket ride, it took him all the way to the moon and back!

Eventually one of the elves said they had to go before daylight came.

Bobby climbed wearily back into the train and soon he was fast asleep. When he woke up it was morning, and he was back in his bed. The train set lay quite still on its tracks. But in one of the carriages was a scrap of paper and on the paper, in tiny spidery writing, were the words:
We hope you enjoyed your trip to Toyland
– the elves.

Smelly Pup

All the animals were gathered in the barn. "It has come to our attention," said Mrs Hen to Smelly Pup, "that you are in need of a bath. You haven't had one all summer. Even the pigs are complaining!"

Smelly Pup just laughed. "Take a bath? That'll be the day!" he said, and off he went.

Outside Smelly Pup strolled through the farmyard, muttering, "What a crazy idea. I'm a dog. I do dog things... like chasing cats!" The farm cat leapt up hissing as Smelly Pup came racing towards her. He chased her all around the farmyard. Then, just as he was about to catch up, she sprang into the air. Smelly Pup took a great leap after her... and landed in the pond with a SPLASH!

"Silly Pup!" smirked the cat as she watched, perched on the branch of a nearby tree.

The ducks quacked as he spluttered and splashed, chasing them through the water! The water felt cool and refreshing on his fur. After a while, he came out and rolled on the nice muddy bank. "That was fun," he said. "Maybe I could get used to baths after all!"

A Spelling Lesson!

Wanda Witch went wandering through a very spooky wood. She loved to practise spooky spells, and the thought of doing anything good made her feel really ill.

She took great delight in turning a patch of beautiful bluebells into a pool of smelly, slimy goo. Then she gave a tree a creepy face that would frighten anyone who happened to be passing.

Creeping through the undergrowth, Wanda came upon a wizard, standing gazing into a pond. As quick as lightning, she waved her wand and the wizard fell straight into the water! Although the water wasn't very deep, it was very cold and full of horrible, slimy weeds.

The wizard leapt out in one huge jump, and was so angry with Wanda that he cast a spell as he landed next to her. His big red cloak wrapped itself around Wanda's body. Then it began to squeeze her really tight.

"Say sorry!" roared the wizard, "or you will stay like that!"

Wanda was shocked to have met someone who was even speedier and nastier than her! She apologised hastily to the wizard, and promised that from now on there would be no more nasty spells!

Witch's Brew

Winnie Witch was having a wonderful time! From her kitchen, deep inside a dark cave, came the sound of bubbling and singing as she stood stirring her huge cauldron. She was singing the spell for a magic monster as she threw the ingredients into the pot.

It had taken her days to collect the long list from her book of magic spells. Eye of lizard, toe of frog, tail of rat and bark of dog, sneeze of chicken, lick of weasel and smell of cat were all easy – but the cough of bat had been hard. Winnie had to chase a bat on her broomstick! It whizzed through the night sky so fast that Winnie thought she would fall off her broomstick. Eventually the bat must have choked on a fly. It coughed, spluttered, and slowed down. Winnie scooped up a cough and put it in her pocket before returning home for a rest!

The cauldron began to bubble furiously as Winnie stirred faster. Then… a monster's head began rising out of the pot.

"Ah!" sighed Winnie, "very pleased to meet you!"

"Mmm! Very pleased to *eat* you!" replied the monster!

Winnie went pale. Surely this wasn't right! She grabbed her wand and frantically shook it at the monster, whispering a spell. With a whoosh and a bang, the monster disappeared. Winnie won't be trying that spell again!

The Three Jovial Welshmen

One, Two, Three, Four, Five

One, two, three, four, five,
   Once I caught a fish alive;
Six, seven, eight, nine, ten,
   Then I let him go again.
Why did you let him go?
   Because he bit my finger so.
Which finger did he bite?
   This little finger on the right.

There were three jovial Welshmen,
   As I have heard them say,
And they would go a-hunting
   Upon St David's day.

All the day they hunted,
   And nothing could they find
But a ship a-sailing,
   A-sailing with the wind.

One said it was a ship;
   The other he said nay;
The third said it was a house,
   With the chimney blown away.

And all the night they hunted,
   And nothing could they find
But the moon a-gliding,
   A-gliding with the wind.

Five Little Monkeys

Five little monkeys walked along the shore;
   One went a-sailing,
   Then there were four.
Four little monkeys climbed up a tree;
   One of them tumbled down,
   Then there were three.
Three little monkeys found a pot of glue;
   One got stuck in it,
   Then there were two.
Two little monkeys found a currant bun;
   One ran away with it,
   Then there was one.
One little monkey cried all afternoon,
   So they put him in an aeroplane
   And sent him to the moon.

I Love Sixpence

I love sixpence, pretty little sixpence,
　I love sixpence better than my life;
I spent a penny of it, I spent another,
　And took fourpence home to my wife.

Oh, my little fourpence, pretty little fourpence,
　I love fourpence better than my life;
I spent a penny of it, I spent another,
　And I took twopence home to my wife.

Oh, my little twopence, my pretty little twopence,
　I love twopence better than my life;
I spent a penny of it, I spent another,
　And I took nothing home to my wife.

Oh, my little nothing, my pretty little nothing,
　What will nothing buy for my wife?
I have nothing, I spend nothing,
　I love nothing better than my wife.

Three Young Rats

Three young rats with black felt hats,
　Three young ducks with white straw flats,
Three young dogs with curling tails,
　Three young cats with demi-veils,
Went out to walk with two young pigs
　In satin vests and sorrel wigs;
But suddenly it chanced to rain,
　And so they all went home again.

One, Two, Buckle My Shoe

One, two,
　Buckle my shoe;
Three, four,
　Shut the door;
Five, six,
　Pick up sticks;
Seven, eight,
　Lay them straight;
Nine, ten,
　A good fat hen;

Eleven, twelve,
　Who will delve?
Thirteen, fourteen,
　Maids a-courting;
Fifteen, sixteen,
　Maids a-kissing;
Seventeen, eighteen,
　Maid a-waiting;
Nineteen, twenty,
　My stomach's empty.

Birthday Bunnies

"It's my first birthday tomorrow!" announced Snowy, a little white rabbit, very proudly. "Isn't that exciting?"

"Yes, very exciting!" said Whiskers, her brother. "Because it's my birthday too!"

"And mine!" said Patch.

"And mine!" said Nibble.

"And mine!" said Twitch.

"Do you think Mummy and Daddy have got a surprise for us?" asked Snowy.

"I hope so!" said Whiskers, giggling.

Mrs Rabbit was listening outside the door, as her children were getting ready for bed. She heard the little bunnies chattering excitedly about their birthdays the next day.

Whatever could she do to make it a special day for them? She sat and thought very hard, and later that evening, when Mr Rabbit came home, she said: "It is the children's first birthday tomorrow, and I'm planning a surprise for them. I want to make them a carrot cake, but I will need some carrots. Could you go and dig up some nice fresh ones from your vegetable garden?"

"Certainly, dear," said Mr Rabbit, and off he went back outside.

Mr Rabbit was proud of the carrots he grew. They were very fine carrots — crunchy and delicious. Every year he entered them in the Country Show, and they nearly always won first prize. So you can imagine his dismay when he arrived at his vegetable patch to find that every single carrot had been dug up and stolen!

He marched back to the burrow. "Someone has stolen my carrots!" he told his wife, crossly. "And I am going to find out just who it is!"

And, although it was getting late, he went back outside, and set off to find the naughty person.

First of all he stopped at Hungry Hare's house, and knocked loudly.

"Someone has stolen all my carrots!" Mr Rabbit said. "Do you know who?"

"Oh, yes," said Hungry Hare. "But it wasn't me." And, although Mr Rabbit pressed him, Hungry Hare would say no more.

Next Mr Rabbit went to Sly Fox's house.

"Someone has stolen my carrots!" he said. "Do you know who?"

"Oh, yes," said Sly Fox. "But it wasn't me." And, although Mr Rabbit begged and pleaded with him, Sly Fox would say no more.

So Mr Rabbit marched to Bill Badger's house, and asked if he knew who had taken the carrots.

"Why, yes, in fact I do," said Bill Badger. "But it wasn't me."

And just like the others, he would say no more. It was the same wherever Mr Rabbit went, and, although he got very cross, and stamped his foot, no one would tell him who had stolen his carrots!

"You'll find out soon enough," said Red Squirrel.

So Mr Rabbit went home feeling very puzzled.

"It seems that everyone knows who it was, but no one will tell me!" said Mr Rabbit to his wife.

"Not everyone, dear," she said. "I don't know who it was either. All I know is that it's our children's first birthday tomorrow, and we have no surprise for them." And, feeling very miserable and confused, they went to bed, determined to get to the bottom of the mystery in the morning.

Next day the little bunnies came running into the kitchen, where their parents were having breakfast.

"Happy birthday, everyone!" called Snowy.

"Happy birthday!" cried the other little bunnies.

"Now, it's not much, but I wanted to give each of you a surprise!" Snowy went on. "By the way, I hope you don't mind, Dad." And with that Snowy pulled out a box of juicy carrots, each tied with a bow, and handed one to each of her brothers and sisters.

"Snap!" cried Whiskers, "I had just the same idea!" and he pulled out another box of carrots.

"Me too!" said Patch, and "Me too!" said Nibble. Soon there was a great pile of juicy carrots heaped on the kitchen table.

"So that's what happened to my carrots!" cried Mr Rabbit, in amazement. "I thought they had been stolen!" And when he told the little bunnies the story they laughed till their sides ached. Then Mrs Rabbit put on her apron and shooed them outside.

"Just leave the carrots with me," she said. "I have a birthday surprise of my own in store!"

And so the mystery was solved. It turned out that Hungry Hare had seen the little bunnies creep out one by one, and each dig up a few carrots when they thought no one was looking. He knew it was their birthdays and he guessed what they were doing. He had told the other forest folk, and everyone thought it was a great joke.

Mr Rabbit felt very ashamed that he had been so cross with everyone, when they were really just keeping the secret. And so he invited them for a special birthday tea that afternoon, which the little bunnies thought was a great surprise.

And of course the highlight of the day was when Mrs Rabbit appeared from the kitchen carrying, what else, but an enormous carrot cake!

One Dark Night

Paws tiptoed out into the dark farmyard. Mummy had told him to stay in the barn until he was old enough to go out at night. But he was impatient. He had not gone far when something brushed past his ears. He froze as the fur on his neck began to rise. To his relief it was only a bat – there were plenty of those in the barn.

A loud hoot echoed through the trees – "Toowhit, Toowhoo!" and a great dark shape swooped down and snatched something up. "Just an owl," Paws told himself. "Some of those in the barn too. Nothing to be afraid of!" Creeping nervously on into the darkness, he wondered if this was such a good idea after all. Strange rustlings came from every corner, and he jumped as the old pig gave a loud grunt from the pigsty close by.

Then, all of a sudden, Paws froze in his tracks. Beneath the hen house two eyes glinted in the darkness, as they came creeping towards him. This must be the fox Mummy had warned him of! But to his amazement he saw it was Mummy!

"Back to the barn!" she said sternly, and Paws happily did as he was told. Maybe he would wait until he was older to go out at night, after all!

Staying at Grandma's

Jack hugged his teddy bear tightly, while Mum packed his slippers and pyjamas into a bag.

"Why can't I come with you?" he asked.

"Because Dad and I have to go away for one night," said Mum. "You're going to stay with Gran and Grandad. They can't wait to see you."

"But I'll be scared without you and Dad," whispered Jack.

"Don't worry," said Mum. "You'll have such a good time, you won't want to come home!"

Later that day, Gran and Grandad opened their front door, as Mum, Dad and Jack arrived in their car. Holly, Gran's little dog, peeped through her legs, wagging her tail with excitement. But soon, it was time for Jack to say goodbye to his mum and dad. Jack felt really sad. He didn't want them to leave. He hugged his mum tightly. "I'll miss you," he said.

Mum gave Jack a big hug. "We'll be back tomorrow morning, I promise," she smiled. Then, she and Dad got into the car.

As they drove away, Jack waved until he couldn't see the car any more. His eyes filled with tears. "Come on, Jack," said Gran, giving him a big cuddle. "We're going to have such a good time. Guess where Grandad's taking us this afternoon?" Jack wiped his eyes and shook his head.

"Um... I don't know," he sniffed. Grandad gave him a tissue. Just then, Holly came bounding over. "Hello, Holly," said Jack, looking more cheerful. He rubbed her big, floppy ears. Jack loved Holly and, just for tonight, he could pretend she was his dog.

"Grandad," asked Jack, "where are we going this afternoon?"

"It's a surprise," said Grandad. "But we'll need the car. Why don't we give it a good clean?" So, Grandad gave Jack a big, yellow sponge and a bucket of soapy water. Soon, bubbles filled the air. They even went on Holly's nose!

Just then, Gran called to Jack from the kitchen. "I'm going to make a lovely picnic to take with us," said Gran. "Would you like to help me, Jack?" Jack nodded. At home, he liked to help his mum, too. "Grandad likes sausage rolls and I like cheese and tomato sandwiches," said Gran. "What's your favourite food?"

"Chocolate spread sandwiches!" said Jack, licking his lips. "Can we take something for Holly, too?"

"Of course," said Gran, smiling. "She can have one of her crunchy biscuits."

When the car was clean and the picnic was ready, Jack and Grandad packed everything for their trip into the boot.

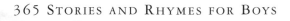
Then, Gran strapped Jack into his car seat and they all set off.

"Here we are," said Grandad. "The park."

"Great!" said Jack. He couldn't wait to get out and explore. They soon found the perfect place for their picnic. Jack hungrily ate his chocolate sandwiches.

Afterwards, Grandad took Jack and Holly for a walk in the woods, while Gran had a little nap. On the way, Jack saw a playground. "Can we go there, Grandad?" he asked.

"Of course we can," said Grandad. First, Grandad pushed Jack on the swings and then watched him zoom down the slide.

"Wheee!" cried Jack. "This is great fun!" Soon, he was laughing and playing with all the other children, while Grandad watched, just like Jack's mum and dad would do.

When it was time to go home, Gran packed up the picnic things and Grandad put them back in the car. Jack was very tired and soon fell asleep. What a fun day they'd had.

That evening, Gran made Jack a special dinner – sausages and mash, followed by apple pie and ice cream.

Afterwards, they watched Jack's favourite television programmes, until it was time for bed. As Jack settled himself in bed, with his teddy bear beside him, Grandad asked him what story he would like. "Mum usually reads me this one," said Jack, picking up a book and handing it to Grandad.

"Once upon a time… " began Grandad. Jack knew the story off by heart. It was nice to hear it again, and soon he was drifting off to sleep. It was just like being at home.

When Jack woke up, he couldn't understand why his room felt so strange. Then, he remembered. He was staying with Gran and Grandad!

"Breakfast, Jack," said Gran, as she came in to help him dress. "Did you sleep well?"

"Yes, thank you, Gran," he said.

For breakfast, Gran cooked Jack a boiled egg, with toasted bread soldiers, milk and fresh orange juice. Delicious!

Afterwards, Jack helped Gran to pack his bag, ready for when Mum and Dad came to collect him. Jack was really excited when he saw his mum and dad arrive. He ran out to meet them and gave them both a giant hug. "Jack!" cried Mum. "Have you had a good time?"

"Yes," laughed Jack. "We went to the park and had a picnic and I played on a slide and had chocolate sandwiches and we took Holly for a walk… and Grandad read me my favourite story. Can I stay again?" Everyone laughed and Holly barked.

"Of course, you can!" said Mum and Dad.

Custard's New Home

Custard the little hippo lived where it was very hot. His home was a cool river that flowed into the sea. This was where he met Sid, the hermit crab. Sid and Custard were best friends.

This was a bit odd because they were as different as could be. Custard was a lot bigger than Sid for a start. Custard thought that being a hermit crab must be really cool. Instead of having one shell like ordinary crabs, they keep changing from one shell to another.

At the moment Sid had a bright pink, pointed shell. He carried it around with him everywhere he went. Custard thought this was really great. He wanted to carry his own home around with him! Then he wouldn't have to stay out in the hot sun. Hippos don't like getting hot. But there are no shells as big as a hippo. So they have to stay in the river to keep cool.

"Will you help me build my own home?" Custard asked Sid one day.

"Of course I will," said Sid. So they built a house of leaves and tied it to Custard's back. Custard was as pleased as could be. They went for a walk by the river. Sid wore a new round blue shell this time. He said it was the latest fashion. They passed a lion that had a bad cold. ATISHOO! The lion sneezed loudly and blew Custard's new house away!

"Bother!" said Custard.

So they built another house, this time of bamboo.

"This won't blow away," said Custard.

But an elephant appeared. And, oh dear! Bamboo is an elephant's favourite food.

"Yummy!" said the elephant. "Thanks for bringing me my breakfast!" And he stuffed Custard's house into his mouth!

"That was my new home," said Custard crossly.

"Oops! Sorry," said the elephant.

Sid was looking for a new home for himself. The blue one was getting too small. He thought a yellow one would be nice. A large bird flying lazily overhead spotted Sid without his shell.

"Ah, crab lunch!" it said, and, swooping low, it grabbed Sid in its claws. Sid wriggled and freed himself. He dropped to the ground with a thump.

Custard rushed to help, but was too big and slow. Looking round, he spotted a deckchair, a sunshade and a bucket and spade.

"Quick," he called to Sid, "over here!" Sid dived under the bucket. Just in time! The bird squawked angrily, and flew away. Custard wriggled his bottom into the stripy deck chair, and settled down under the shade of the green umbrella. It felt nice and cool.

If only his head and legs didn't stick out in front. He wriggled a bit more trying to get comfortable.

"Sid, I've been thinking. I'll just keep cool in the river like I did before," said Custard.

"And I think I'll look for another shell," said Sid.

The two friends wandered back down to the river, happy to be going home together.

Humpty Dumpty

Humpty Dumpty sat on a wall,
 Humpty Dumpty had a great fall;
All the king's horses and all the king's men
 Couldn't put Humpty together again.

We're All in the Dumps

We're all in the dumps,
 For diamonds and trumps,
The kittens are gone to St Paul's,
 The babies are bit,
 The moon's in a fit,
And the houses are built without walls.

Daffy-Down-Dilly

Daffy-Down-Dilly
 Has come up to town
In a yellow petticoat
 And a green gown.

Tweedle-dum and Tweedle-dee

Tweedle-dum and Tweedle-dee
 Agreed to have a battle,
For Tweedle-dum said Tweedle-dee
 Had spoiled his nice new rattle.
Just then flew down a monstrous crow,
 As big as a tar-barrel,
Which frightened both the heroes so,
 They quite forgot their quarrel.

Cushy Cow Bonny

Cushy cow bonny, let down thy milk,
    And I will give thee a gown of silk;
A gown of silk and a silver tee,
    If thou wilt let down thy milk for me.

Hector Protector

Hector Protector was dressed all in green;
    Hector Protector was sent to the Queen.
The Queen did not like him,
    Nor more did the King;
So Hector Protector
    Was sent back again.

Higglety, Pigglety, Pop!

Higglety, Pigglety, pop!
    The dog has eaten the mop;
The pig's in a hurry,
    The cat's in a flurry,
Higglety, pigglety, pop!

There was a Piper

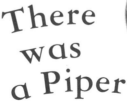

There was a piper, he'd a cow,
    And he'd no hay to give her;
He took his pipes and played a tune:
    "Consider, old cow, consider!"

The cow considered very well,
    For she gave the piper a penny,
That he might play the tune again,
    Of "Corn rigs are bonnie".

Ducks for a Day

One hot, sunny day, Becky and Bobby Chick waddled out of the farmyard, in search of some fun. They wandered down to the stream, where they saw Duck swimming by. "Be careful by the water, chicks," she quacked, cheerily.

"We will, Duck," said Becky, as she watched the big duck swim gracefully past. "Oh, I wish we could swim, Bobby. It must be nice to be a duck."

Mummy had said that they mustn't play by the stream but, when the little chicks spotted a large leaf bobbing gently up and down in the reeds, they just had to hop on for a game. "Let's pretend we're ducks!" laughed Bobby.

The two little chicks played happily on the leaf all morning. "Quack, quack! I wish we could paddle far away like real ducks!" laughed Bobby, jumping up and down. Suddenly, the leaf broke free of the reeds and started to float downstream!

"On, no!" cried Bobby, looking very worried. "How are we going to get off?"

"We'll have to swim!" sobbed Becky.

"But we can't!" said Bobby. "We're not real ducks! Help! Help!" The leaf-boat floated

gently downstream, past the meadow where all the animals from Buttercup Farm were grazing.

"Don't worry, Becky, the farm animals will save us!" cheeped Bobby, waving his wing, trying to get the animals' attention. "Help!"

"Oh look everyone!" mooed Cow. "The little chicks are waving to us!" All the animals laughed and waved their tails back – everyone except Duck. She could see the chicks' frightened faces, as well as the waterfall up ahead! The chicks were in danger. "They're not waving!" she cried. "They're floating away!"

Duck leapt into the water and began paddling after the chicks, as fast as she could! When she reached the leaf she tried to pull it to the bank but the current was too strong and they were getting closer and closer to the waterfall.

Then, Duck had an idea. "Quick," she quacked to the two chicks. "Hop on to my back!" Becky and Bobby leapt on to Duck's back, then Duck swam back upstream to safety.

When they reached the farm, they jumped off Duck's back and thanked her for saving them. Mummy Hen was waiting, anxiously. "We're so sorry, Mummy!" cried Becky, rushing over to her. "We'll never disobey you again!"

"It was nice being a duck for a while!" sniffed Bobby. "But being a chick is better!"

"And much safer!" clucked Mummy Hen, giving them both a big hug.

Monkey Mayhem

Mickey and Maxine Monkey had finished their breakfast of Mango Munch. Now they were rushing off to play.

"Be careful!" called their mum. "And please DON'T make too much noise!"

"We won't!" the two mischievous monkeys promised, leaping across to the next tree.

"Wheeee," screeched Mickey, and "Wa-hoooo!" hollered Maxine.

The noise echoed through the whole jungle – Mickey and Maxine just didn't know how to be quiet!

Ka-thunk! Mickey landed on a branch. Ka-clunk! Maxine landed beside him. Ker-aack!

"Ooohh noooo!" the monkeys hollered as the branch snapped.

"Yi-i-i-kes!" they shrieked, as they went tumbling down. Ker-thumpp! The jungle shook as the two monkeys crashed to the ground.

"Yipppeeee!" the monkeys cheered, jumping up happily.

"That was so much FUN!" exclaimed Maxine. "Let's go and get Chico Chimp and see if he wants to do it, too!" And the two monkeys scrambled back up to the tree tops, bellowing, "HEY, CHICO! COME AND PLAY WITH US!" as they swung through the branches.

All over the jungle, animals shook their heads and covered their ears. Couldn't anyone keep those naughty, noisy monkeys quiet?

Chico Chimp arrived to play with his friends. The three of them were having a great time swinging, tumbling and bouncing together when suddenly they stopped short. Grandpa Gorilla was standing in their path, glaring at them angrily.

"Go away, you mischief-makers," he said. "You've given us all enough headaches today. My grandson Gulliver is fast asleep by the river and, if you wake him up, I will be very, very upset!"

"Sorry," whispered Maxine, looking down at the ground. Everyone in the jungle knew it was a big mistake to upset Grandpa Gorilla!

"We'll be quiet," they promised.

Mickey, Maxine and Chico didn't know what to do until Mickey said, "Let's climb the coconut palm tree. We can do that quietly."

"Okay," the others agreed half-heartedly.

"I suppose it's better than doing nothing," said Maxine.

From their perch among the coconuts, the three friends could see right over the jungle.

They saw Jerome Giraffe showing his son Jeremy how to choose the juiciest, most tender leaves on a tree… and they saw Portia Parrot giving her daughter Penelope her first flying lesson. And right down below them, they saw little Gulliver Gorilla sleeping contentedly in the tall grass beside the river.

And – uh-oh! They saw something else, too… Claudia Crocodile was in the river. She was grinning and snapping her big, sharp teeth – and heading straight for Gulliver!

The friends didn't think twice. Maxine shouted, "GET UP, GULLIVER! GET UP RIGHT NOOOOOOWW!"

Then Mickey and Chico began throwing coconuts at Claudia.

SMAACCCK! they went, on Claudia's hard crocodile head.

"OWW-WOOW!" moaned Claudia.

"What's going on here?" Grandpa Gorilla shouted up into the coconut tree. "I thought I told you three to keep quiet!"

All the noise woke Gulliver. The little gorilla sat up, looked around, and ran to his grandpa, who was hurrying towards the river.

When Grandpa saw Claudia he realised what had happened. "I am so glad you're safe!" he said, giving Gulliver a great big gorilla hug. The three monkeys came down from the tree.

"We're sorry we made so much noise," Chico said.

By this time all the gorillas had gathered around, and so had most of the other animals.

"What's going on?" squawked Portia Parrot.

"Yes, what's all the commotion about?" asked Jerome Giraffe.

"These three youngsters are heroes," said Grandpa. "They have saved my grandson from being eaten by Claudia Crocodile!"

"I think you all deserve a reward," said Grandpa. "And I think it should be…"

"Hurrah!" cheered all the other animals and then they held their breath in anticipation.

"…permission to be just as noisy as you like, whenever you like!" Grandpa Gorilla announced.

"YIPPEEE!" cheered Mickey, Maxine and Chico, in their loudest, screechiest voices. Their grins were almost as wide as the river.

"OH, NOOOOO!" all the other animals groaned together – but they were all smiling, too.

Lizzie and the Tractor

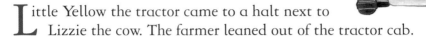

Little Yellow the tractor came to a halt next to Lizzie the cow. The farmer leaned out of the tractor cab.

"Come on Lizzie, get up!" said the farmer. "We have the big farm show in one week. How are you going to win the Best Cow prize if you laze around all day getting plump? You're so lazy!"

"I like lying here!" said Lizzie the cow. "I have all the grass I need right here next to me. I don't even have to get up!"

"Wouldn't you like to be pride of the show, Lizzie?" wailed the farmer.

"No!" said Lizzie, as she munched on her mouthful and thought about it.

The farmer did not know what to do. All his animals won prizes except Lizzie. Perhaps they would know how to make Lizzie fit and lovely again.

He drove Little Yellow around the farm to ask their advice. Gorgeous the pig said, "She is too dull! Paint her pink with brown spots… it always works for me."

Reckless the goat said, "She eats too much grass. Get her to eat newspapers… it always works for me!"

Flash the cockerel said, "Her tail is too small. Stick lots of big bright feathers on her bottom… it always works for me!" Then Little Yellow said, "I can make Lizzie into the Best Cow again."

The animals snorted with laughter. How could a tractor do anything they could not? But the farmer just said, "Please do everything you can, Little Yellow!"

So Little Yellow bustled around in his barn, humming to himself and trying on all the bits and pieces that a tractor can make use of. First he put on his big bulldozer bucket and went over to Lizzie.

"Please Lizzie, move into the small field."

"Shan't!" said Lizzie, rolling on to her back.

So Little Yellow scooped her up and took her into the field in the bucket. "It's for your own good," said Little Yellow.

Then Little Yellow put on his plough and, to everyone's amazement, ploughed up the grass in the middle of the field.

Next day, Little Yellow ploughed another strip in the middle of the field, and the day after that too. The ploughed bit was getting bigger and the grassy bit was getting smaller.

Lizzie cried, "There's not enough grass left to eat! I'm getting thinner!"

Then Little Yellow put on his grass cutter. He mowed all the grass that was left. If Lizzie lay down again she would not get enough to eat. She was smaller now, and the exercise was making her coat glossy.

But the tractor was not finished. He put on his back forks and took Lizzie a bale of hay to eat but, as she rushed to eat it, he drove away, and she had to trot behind to keep up. By the end of the day she was very tired, but fit and healthy too.

By this time, Little Yellow had used nearly every tool he had! The last thing he used was a power spray to wash her down, and... Ta-ra!... there stood Lizzie, more beautiful than ever before!

Lizzie went to the show, and of course was declared Best Cow. The farmer was given a silver cup to put on his sideboard. And all thanks to Little Yellow the tractor!

The Littlest Pig

Little Pig had a secret. He snuggled down in the warm hay with his brothers and sisters, looked up at the dark sky twinkling with stars, and smiled a secret smile to himself. Maybe it wasn't so bad being the littlest pig after all...

Not so long ago, Little Pig had been feeling quite fed up. He was the youngest and the smallest pig in the family. He had five brothers and five sisters who were all much bigger and fatter than him. The farmer's wife called him Runt, because he was the smallest pig of the litter.

His brothers and sisters teased him terribly. "Poor little Runtie," they said to him, giggling. "You must be the smallest pig in the world!"

"Leave me alone!" said Little Pig, and he crept off to the corner of the pigpen, where he curled into a ball, and started to cry. "If you weren't all so greedy, and let me have some food, maybe I'd be bigger!" he mumbled, sadly.

Every feeding time was the same – the others all pushed and shoved, until all that was left was the scraps. He would never grow bigger at this rate.

Then one day Little Pig made an important discovery. He was hiding in the corner of the pen, as usual, when he spied a little hole in the fence tucked away behind the feeding trough.

"I could fit through there!" thought Little Pig.

He waited all day until it was time for bed, and then, when he was sure that all of his brothers and sisters were fast asleep, he wriggled through the hole. Suddenly he was outside, free to go wherever he pleased. And what an adventure he had!

First, he ran to the hen house and gobbled up the bowls of grain. Then he ran to the field and crunched up Donkey's carrots.

He ran to the vegetable patch and munched a row of cabbages. What a feast! Then, when he was full to bursting, he headed for home. On the way he stopped by the hedgerow. What was that lovely smell? He rooted around and found where it was coming from – a bank of wild strawberries.

Little Pig had never tasted anything quite so delicious.

"Tomorrow night, I'll start with these!" he

promised himself as he trotted back home to the pigpen. He wriggled back through the hole, and fell fast asleep snuggled up to his mother, smiling very contentedly.

Every night Little Pig continued his tasty adventures. He didn't mind when they pushed him out of the way at feeding time, he knew that a much better feast awaited him outside. Sometimes he would find the dog's bowl filled with scraps from the farmer's supper, or buckets of oats ready for the horses. "Yum, yum – piggy porridge!" he would giggle, and gobbled it up.

But, as the days and weeks went by, and Little Pig grew bigger and fatter, every night it became more of a squeeze to wriggle and push his way through the hole.

Little Pig knew that soon he would no longer be able to fit through the hole, but by then he would be big enough to stand up to his brothers and sisters. And for now he was enjoying his secret!

Making a Splash!

One day, Mrs Hen and her chicks were walking near the pond, when Mrs Duck swam by, followed by a line of ducklings. The ducklings were playing games as they swam along. They chased each other around and ducked down under the water.

"Can we play in the water too?" the chicks asked Mrs Hen. "It looks like fun!"

"Oh, no, dears," said Mrs Hen. "Chicks and water don't mix! You haven't got the right feathers or feet!"

This made the chicks very miserable. "It's not fair!" they grumbled. "We wish we were ducklings!"

On the way home, a big black cloud appeared and it started to rain. Soon the chicks' fluffy feathers were wet through.

They scurried back to the hen house as fast as they could and arrived wet, cold and shivering. They quickly snuggled under their mothers' wings and they were soon feeling better. Their feathers were dry and fluffy in no time at all.

"Imagine being wet all the time!" said the chicks. "Thank goodness we're not ducklings, after all!"

Betty Pringle

Betty Pringle had a little pig,
  Not very little and not very big;
When he was alive he lived in clover;
  But now he's dead, and that's all over.
So Billy Pringle,
  he laid down and cried,
And Betty Pringle,
  she laid down and died;
So there was an end of one,
  two, and three:
Billy Pringle he,
  Betty Pringle she,
And the piggy wiggy.

If Wishes Were Horses

If wishes were horses,
  Beggars would ride;
If turnips were watches,
  I'd wear one by my side.

Jack be Nimble

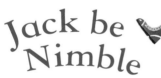

Jack be nimble,
  And Jack be quick:
And Jack jump over
  The candlestick.

As I Walked by Myself

As I walked by myself,
  And talked to myself,
Myself said unto me,
  Look to thyself,
  Take care of thyself,
For nobody cares for thee.

I answered myself,
  And said to myself,
In the self-same repartee,
  Look to thyself,
  Or not look to thyself,
The self-same thing will be.

Yankee Doodle

Yankee Doodle went to town,
    Riding on a pony;
He stuck a feather in his hat,
    And called it macaroni.
Yankee Doodle fa, so, la,
    Yankee Doodle dandy,
Yankee Doodle fa, so, la,
    Buttermilk and brandy.

Yankee Doodle went to town
    To buy a pair of trousers,
He swore he could not see the town
    For so many houses.
Yankee Doodle fa, so, la,
    Yankee Doodle dandy,
Yankee Doodle fa, so, la,
    Buttermilk and brandy.

If All the World was Apple-pie

If all the world was apple-pie,
    And all the sea was ink,
And all the trees were bread and cheese,
    What should we have for drink?

Fire on the Mountain

Rats in the garden – catch'em Towser!
    Cows in the cornfield – run boys run!
Cat's in the cream pot – stop her now, sir!
    Fire on the mountain – run boys run!

The Man in the Wilderness

The man in the wilderness asked me,
    How many strawberries grew in the sea?
I answered him as I thought good,
    As many red herrings as grew in the wood.

Take the Ghost Train

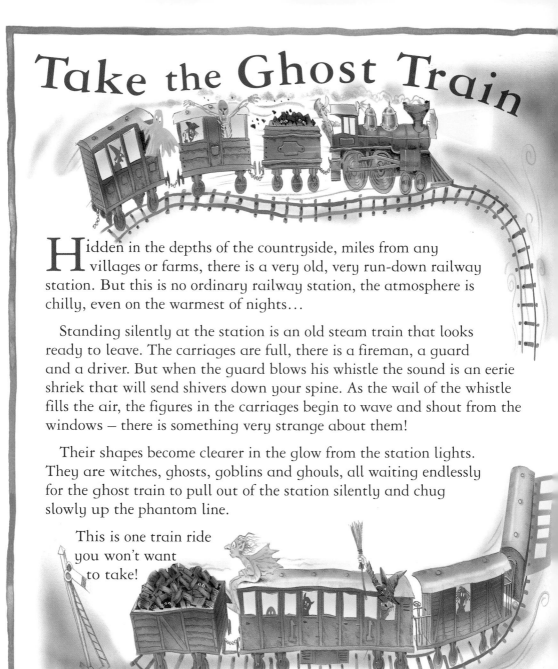

Hidden in the depths of the countryside, miles from any villages or farms, there is a very old, very run-down railway station. But this is no ordinary railway station, the atmosphere is chilly, even on the warmest of nights...

Standing silently at the station is an old steam train that looks ready to leave. The carriages are full, there is a fireman, a guard and a driver. But when the guard blows his whistle the sound is an eerie shriek that will send shivers down your spine. As the wail of the whistle fills the air, the figures in the carriages begin to wave and shout from the windows – there is something very strange about them!

Their shapes become clearer in the glow from the station lights. They are witches, ghosts, goblins and ghouls, all waiting endlessly for the ghost train to pull out of the station silently and chug slowly up the phantom line.

This is one train ride you won't want to take!

Ode to Ghosts

You may not know this, but the life of a castle ghost is very sad. He spends his days haunting cold, lonely rooms and corridors, and on birthdays and at Christmas time the postman never arrives with cards and parcels for him.

All day long the ghost floats from one room to another. He howls and clanks his chains, but most people blame the noise on the wind outside or the ancient drains. Occasionally he might appear when everyone is sitting eating their supper in the hope of a snack and a chat, but everyone screams and runs away. Naturally this doesn't make him feel any better.

What is even worse, the poor ghost has to wander around all night while everyone else is tucked up in bed! He would really like a warm bed to sleep in – but as soon as anyone wakes up they scream and shout so loudly that the ghost feels embarrassed and slips away.

So, the next time you see a ghost wafting along a castle corridor, don't run away in fright. Stay a while and have a chat, you'll find him most polite!

Lazy Teddy

There was nothing Lazy Teddy liked more than to be tucked up snug and warm in Joshua's bed.

Every morning the alarm clock would ring and Joshua would leap out of bed and fling open the curtains. "I love mornings!" he'd say, stretching his arms up high as the sun poured in through the window. "You're crazy!" Teddy would mutter, and he'd burrow down beneath the quilt to the bottom of the bed, where he'd spend the rest of the morning snoozing happily.

"Come out and play, you lazy bear," Joshua would call. But Lazy Teddy wouldn't budge. He would just snore even louder.

Joshua wished that Teddy would be more lively, like his other friends' bears. He loved having adventures, but they would be even better if Teddy would share them with him.

One evening, Joshua decided to have a talk with Teddy before they went to bed. He told him about the fishing trip he'd been on that day with his friends and their teddy bears.

"It was lots of fun, Teddy. I wish you'd been there. It really is time you stopped being such a lazybones. Tomorrow is my birthday, and I'm having a party. There will be games, and presents and ice cream. Please promise you'll come?"

"It does sound like fun," said Teddy. "Okay, I promise. I'll get up just this once."

The next morning, Joshua was up bright and early. "Yippee, it's my birthday today!" he yelled, dancing around the room. He pulled the covers off his bed. "Come on, Teddy, time to get up!"

"Just five more minutes!" groaned Teddy, and he rolled over and fell straight back to sleep. When Joshua came back up to his room after breakfast, Teddy still wasn't up. Well, by now Joshua was getting quite cross with Teddy. He reached over and poked him in the tummy. Teddy opened one eye and growled. "Wake up, Teddy! You promised, remember?" said Joshua.

Teddy yawned. "Oh, if I must!" he said, and muttering and grumbling he climbed out of bed. He washed his face and paws, brushed his teeth

and put on his best red waistcoat.

"There, I'm ready!" he said.

"Good," said Joshua. "About time too!"

Just then the doorbell rang, and Joshua ran to answer it. "I'll come and fetch you in a minute," he said to Teddy. But when he returned there was no sign of Teddy, just a gentle snoring coming from the bottom of the bed.

Joshua was so cross and upset with Lazy Teddy, that he decided to leave him right where he was.

"He'll just have to miss the party!" he said. Deep down though, he was hurt that Teddy wouldn't keep his promise.

Joshua enjoyed his party, although he wished that Teddy had been there. Later that night when he got into bed, he lay crying quietly into his pillow.

LAZY TEDDY

Teddy lay awake in the dark, listening. He knew Joshua was crying because he had let him down, and he felt very ashamed.

"I'm sorry!" whispered Lazy Teddy, and he snuggled up to Joshua and stroked him with a paw until he fell asleep.

The next morning when the alarm clock rang, Joshua leapt out of bed, as usual. But what was this? Teddy had leapt out of bed too, and was stretching his paws up high. Joshua looked at him in amazement.

"What are we doing today, then?" asked Teddy.

"G...g...going for a picnic," stammered Joshua, in surprise. "Are you coming?"

"Of course," said Teddy. And from that day on, Teddy was up bright and early every day, ready to enjoy another day of adventures with Joshua, and he never let him down again.

All at Sea

It was a lovely spring day when Dippy Duckling peeked out of her warm nest at the shimmering river. How cool and inviting the water looked. Soon she was swimming along happily, calling out to all the animals that lived on the riverbank as she went by. She didn't realise how fast or how far the current was carrying her as she swept along past forests and fields.

As Dippy floated on enjoying the warm sun on her back Sally Seagull flew by, squawking loudly. "I've never seen a bird like that on the river before," thought Dippy, in surprise. Then, just as she came round a great bend in the river, she saw the wide, shining ocean spread out in front of her! Dippy began to shake with terror – she was going to be swept out to sea! She started to paddle furiously against the tide, but it was no use. The

current was too strong. Just then, a friendly face popped up nearby. It was Ollie Otter. He was very surprised to find Dippy so far from home.

"Climb on my back," he said. Soon his strong legs were pulling them back up the river and safely home.

"Thank you, Ollie," said Dippy. "Without you, I'd be all at sea!"

Benny the Barmy Builder

Benny was a hard-working builder, and he always did his very best. But sometimes he could be forgetful!

One morning, Benny the Builder arrived bright and early at Vicky Vet's surgery. "Benny the Builder at your service!" he announced. "I think you have a job for me to do."

"Not me, Benny," replied Vicky. "But Polly Postlady has!"

"Of course!" said Benny. "Sorry – I really shouldn't be so forgetful!"

And off he went to Polly Postlady's house. "Benny the Builder at your service!" Benny announced. "Woof!" said Benny's dog, Rocky.

"Come in," called Polly.

She took out a drawing to show Benny.

"I want you to build a Wendy house in my garden," Polly said. "It's a surprise for my grandchildren, Peter, Penny and Patty. I did this drawing to show you just how it should look."

Benny and Polly looked at the drawing together.

"The Wendy house should have two tall doors," said Polly, "one at the front and one at the back, with one small step at the back door. There should be five windows, one at either side of the front door and one on each of the other sides."

"Yes, I see," said Benny.

"And I want a nice sloping roof," said Polly, "not a flat roof!"

"Yes, I see," said Benny. "I will do my very best!"

Polly left for the post office, and Benny went out to start work. But he had barely begun when a gust of wind came along. WHOOSH! went Polly's drawing, up in the air. "WOOF!" barked Rocky, leaping up to catch it.

Oh no! The drawing got caught in the branches of a tree!

Rocky fetched the drawing but, by the time Benny got it back, it was in shreds.

"Oh dear!" moaned Benny the Builder. "How will I build the Wendy house now?"

Benny tried to remember

everything in the drawing. But he quickly got very confused!

"Was it five windows and two doors with one step?" Benny puzzled. "Or was it two windows and five doors with three steps? Was the roof flat and not sloping? Or sloping and not flat? Were the doors tall or small? Oh dear, oh dear!"

Benny decided that he would just have to do the best he could. He got to work measuring… mixing… laying bricks… sawing wood… hammering nails… fixing screws… plastering and painting… and doing his very best to make everything just right.

Late that afternoon, Polly Postlady got home from work. She couldn't wait to see what Benny had done. But, what a surprise she had! The Wendy house's roof was flat. The bottom of the house was sloping. There were two steps leading up to two doors on one side of the house and there were two floors, both different sizes. And there were two windows on one side of the house.

"It's all wrong!" said Polly to Benny. "How will you ever fix it in time?"

But Benny didn't have a chance to answer because, just at that moment, Polly's grandchildren arrived.

"Oooh! Look! A Wendy house!" they cried happily as they rushed towards it. "There's a door for each of us!" they all cried together.

"And we can climb right up to the roof!" said Patty.

"And slide down the other side!" said Peter.

"And there are loads of windows so it's nice and bright inside!" said Penny.

"Granny, it's the best Wendy house ever!" the children told Polly.

"It is perfect. Thank you so much!"

"Well, I think you should thank Benny the Builder," said Polly Postlady, smiling. Benny the Builder smiled too. "I just did my very best," he said.

Tiger Tricks

Tiger loved to play tricks. Every time he found a new one, he couldn't wait to try it out on all of his friends. His latest one was – tying knots!

So, when Elephant was sleeping, Tiger tied a knot in his trunk! When Monkey was dozing, Tiger tied a knot in his tail! And when Snake was snoozing, Tiger tied a knot in – Snake!

Tiger thought it was great fun. The other animals didn't – they were fed up with Tiger, and his tricks.

"I've had enough of this!" said Elephant, rubbing his sore trunk.

"Something has to be done," said Monkey, rubbing his sore tail.

"He's gone too far this time!" said sore Snake.

"We need to catch him before he can try out his tricks on us," said Monkey.

"But that's the problem," said Snake. "We never see him coming in time."

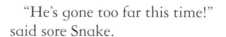

The others agreed. They never spotted Tiger sneaking up on them because, in the

jungle, Tiger's stripes made him really difficult to see! So all the animals thought really hard. Monkey scratched his head. Snake wriggled and writhed and Elephant swung his trunk.

Suddenly Elephant said, "I've got an idea!" He led them all to a fruit tree near the water hole.

When Elephant had explained his plan, a huge smile spread across Monkey's face, and Snake began to snigger. Monkey quickly scampered up the tree, and carried down some of the bright red fruits. Snake wriggled around in the soft earth, until he made a smooth hollow. Then Elephant squeezed the fruits with his trunk, until the bright red juice filled the hollow that Snake had made – and then the animals waited.

It wasn't long before Tiger came strolling along to the water hole, giggling. He started drinking...

Elephant dipped his trunk into the fruit juice and sucked hard. Then he pointed his trunk at Tiger and blew. The juice flew across the clearing, spattering Tiger all over, soaking into his coat. He looked as if he had bright red spots! Tiger jumped with shock.

"That'll take weeks to wear off," Elephant laughed.

"Yes, we'll see you coming for miles," said Monkey.

"So you won't be able to sneak up on us and play any more tricks," added Snake.

And all the animals laughed – except for bright red Tiger!

This Little Piggy

This little piggy went to market,
  This little piggy stayed at home,
This little piggy had roast beef,
  This little piggy had none,
And this little piggy cried,
  Wee-wee-wee-wee-wee,
All the way home.

To Market, to Market, to Buy a Fat Pig

To market, to market, to buy a fat pig,
  Home again, home again, dancing a jig;
Ride to the market to buy a fat hog,
  Home again, home again, jiggety-jog.

To Market, to Market

To market, to market,
  To buy a plum bun;
Home again, home again,
  Market is done.

Jim Crow

Twist about, turn about,
  Jump Jim Crow;
Every time I wheel about
  I do just so.

Two Little Men in a Flying Saucer

Two little men in a flying saucer
  Flew round the world one day.
They looked to the left and right a bit
  And couldn't bear the sight of it,
And then they flew away!

I Can ...

I can tie my shoe lace,
  I can brush my hair,
I can wash my hands and face
  And dry myself with care.

I can clean my teeth too,
  And fasten up my frocks.
I can say, "How do you do?"
  And pull up both my socks.

Higgledy Piggledy

Higgledy piggledy,
  Here we lie,
Picked and plucked,
  And put in a pie!

Two Fat Gentlemen

Two fat gentlemen met in a lane,
  Bowed most politely, bowed once again.
How do you do? How do you do?
  How do you do again?

Two thin ladies met in a lane,
  Bowed most politely, bowed once again.
How do you do? How do you do?
  How do you do again?

Two tall policemen met in a lane,
  Bowed most politely, bowed once again.
How do you do? How do you do?
  How do you do again?

Two little schoolboys met in a lane,
  Bowed most politely, bowed once again.
How do you do? How do you do?
  How do you do again?

Tumbling

In jumping and tumbling
  We spend the whole day,
Till night by arriving
  Has finished our play.

What then? One and all,
  There's no more to be said,
As we tumbled all day,
  So we tumble to bed.

Lie a-Bed

Lie a-bed,
  Sleepy head,
Shut up eyes, bo-peep;
Till day-break
  Never wake:–
Baby, sleep.

Jack and the Beanstalk

Jack was a lively young boy who lived with his mother in a tiny little cottage in the country.

Jack and his mother were very poor. They had straw on the floor, and many panes of glass in their windows were broken. The only thing of value that was left was a cow.

One day, Jack's mother called him in from the garden, where he was chopping logs for their stove. "You will have to take Daisy the cow to market and sell her," she said sadly.

As Jack trudged along the road to market, he met a strange old man.

"Where are you taking that fine milking cow?" asked the man.

"To market, sir," replied Jack, "to sell her."

"If you sell her to me," said the man, "I will give you these beans. They are special, magic beans. I promise you won't regret it."

When Jack heard the word "magic", he became

very excited. He quickly swapped the cow for the beans, and ran all the way home.

Jack rushed through the cottage door. "Mother! Mother!" he called. "Where are you?"

"Why are you home so soon?" asked Jack's mother, coming down the stairs. "How much did you get for the cow?"

"I got these," said Jack, holding out his hand. "They're magic beans!"

"What?" shrieked his mother. "You sold our only cow for a handful of beans? You silly boy, come here!"

Angrily, she snatched the beans from Jack's hand and flung them out of the window and into the garden. Jack was sent to bed with no supper that night.

The next morning, Jack's rumbling stomach woke him early. His room was strangely dark. As he got dressed, he glanced out of his window – and what he saw took his breath away.

Overnight, a beanstalk had sprung up in the garden. Its trunk was almost as thick as Jack's cottage and its top was so tall that it disappeared into the clouds.

Jack yelled with excitement and rushed outside. As he began to climb the beanstalk, his mother stood at the bottom and begged for him to come back down, but he took no notice.

At last, tired and very hungry, Jack reached the top. He found himself in a strange land full of clouds. He could see something glinting in the

distance and began walking towards it.

Eventually he reached the biggest castle he had ever seen. Maybe he could find some food in the kitchen there?

He crept carefully under the front door and ran straight into an enormous foot!

"What was that?" boomed a female voice, and the whole room shook. Jack found himself looking into a huge eye. Suddenly, he was whisked into the air by a giant hand!

"Who are you?" roared the voice.

"I'm Jack," said Jack, "and I'm tired and hungry. Please can you give me something to eat and a place to rest for a while?"

The giant woman was a kind old lady and took pity on the tiny boy. "Don't make a sound," she whispered. "My husband doesn't like boys and will eat you if he finds you." Then she gave Jack a crumb of warm bread and a thimble full of hot soup.

He was just drinking the last drop when the woman said,

"Quick! Hide in the cupboard! My husband's coming!"

From inside the dark cupboard, Jack could hear the approach of thundering footsteps. Then a deep voice bellowed, *Fee, fie, foe, fum, I smell the blood of an Englishman! Be he alive or be he dead, I'll grind his bones to make my bread!*

Jack peeped out through a knothole in the cupboard door, and saw a huge giant standing beside the table.

"Wife!" shouted the giant. "I can smell a boy in the house!"

"Nonsense, dear," said the giant's wife soothingly. "All you can smell is this lovely dinner I have made for you. Now sit down and eat."

When the giant had gobbled up his dinner and a huge bowl of pudding, he shouted, "Wife! Bring me my gold! I wish to count it!"

Jack saw the giant's wife bring out several enormous sacks of coins. The giant picked one up and a cascade of gold fell onto the table top.

Then Jack watched the giant count the coins, one by one. The giant began to stack them up in piles as he worked.

After a while, he started to yawn, and, not long after, Jack saw that he had fallen asleep. Soon Jack heard very loud snoring!

"It's time I made a move!" Jack said to himself. And, quick as a flash, he leapt out of the cupboard, grabbed a sack of gold, slid down the table leg and ran for the door.

But the giant's wife heard him. "Stop, thief!" she screamed at the top of her voice, which woke her husband. He jumped up in a hurry and ran after Jack, shouting loudly, "Come back!"

Jack ran until he came to the top of the beanstalk. Then, with the giant still after him, he scrambled down as fast as he could.

"Mother!" he called, as he got closer to the ground. "Mother, get the axe, quickly!"

By the time Jack reached the bottom, his mother was there with the axe. She chopped down the beanstalk, and the giant came crashing down with it – he never got up again!

Now that they had the gold, Jack and his mother were very rich. They wouldn't have to worry about anything ever again and they lived happily ever after.

Hide and Seek

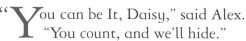

"You can be It, Daisy," said Alex. "You count, and we'll hide."

"Okay," said Daisy. "Poppy can help me to look for you." Poppy was Daisy's new puppy.

"Don't be silly," laughed Sam. "A puppy can't play hide and seek."

"She can because…" began Daisy. But the others weren't listening. They had all run off across the field to hide. "Never mind, Poppy," Daisy told her puppy. "You'll just have to sit here and be good."

Daisy turned round to face the tree. She closed her eyes and began to count. "… ninety-eight, ninety-nine, one hundred." That should have given everyone long enough to hide. Daisy looked round the field. There was no one to be seen. Poppy whined as Daisy ran off towards the hole in the hedge where they had made a den.

She found Sam almost straight away. He was tucked down in a corner of the den. She took him back to the tree. Poppy whined at them. "Dogs can't play hide and seek," Sam told the puppy, and tickled her ear. "You can sit here with me."

Then Daisy found Sarah and Michael just as easily. Emily was harder to find – she was lying very still in the long grass

at the end of the field. Her green T-shirt and trousers made her difficult to see. Daisy took her back to the tree, where the others were all waiting. Poppy whined each time she came back.

"Shhh!" said Daisy. "I won't be long now." But Daisy was wrong – she couldn't find Alex anywhere! Daisy had looked in all their favourite hiding places, but he wasn't in any of them. She didn't know what to do.

"We'll help you to find Alex," said Michael.

So the children searched every corner of the field and every bit of the hedge, but Alex couldn't be found anywhere. Then Poppy began to whine even more loudly.

"She's trying to tell us something," said Daisy. "What is it, Poppy? Show me."

Poppy jumped up. She ran to the tree trunk, leapt up, and began barking. The children all looked up. And there was Alex, sitting on a branch above them, laughing!

"See!" he said. "Daisy was right – puppies can play hide and seek."

Fred the Fearless Fireman

Fireman Fred hurried to the fire station. It was his turn to cook lunch for the firemen on his shift, and he had just bought some nice, plump sausages at the butcher's.

At the fire station, Fred bumped into Builder Benny, who had come to repair a broken window frame.

"Oops! Hello, Benny!" he said. Then he went straight to the kitchen to start cooking. The smell of sausages wafted through the fire station. "Mmm, those sausages smell good!" said Dan and Mike, the other firemen, as they arrived for work. Suddenly the alarm bell rang – CLANG! CLANG! CLANG!

"Emergency!" cried Fireman Mike. He and Fireman Dan rushed down the pole and into their fire-fighting gear. "What about the sausages?" cried Fireman Fred.

"Don't worry about a thing," said Builder Benny, coming in through the window. "I'll look after them till you get back."

"Thanks, Benny!" said Fireman Fred, trying to get his apron off as he rushed down to join the others. The emergency was in Tony's Pizza

Parlour. One of the ovens had caught fire!

"We'll have that blaze out in a jiffy!" said Fred, rushing in with a big fire extinguisher. Dan and Mike followed with the hose.

With a WHIIISH! and a WHOOOSH! from Fred, and a SPLIISH! and a SPLOOOSH! from Mike and Dan, the fire was soon out.

"WHOOPS!" cried Fireman Fred, slipping on the wet floor. But he was back on his feet in a flash. "Thank you!" said Tony, as the firemen took their equipment back to the truck. "I can get back to baking pizzas now!"

Just when they were ready to go back to the station, the firemen heard a call coming through over their radio. "Emergency! Emergency! Window cleaner in distress on Pine Avenue. Emergency! Over..."

"We're on our way!" said Fireman Fred, starting the engine. "Over and out!"

NEE-NAW! NEE-NAW! With sirens blaring, the fire engine zoomed into Pine Avenue. A crowd had gathered around Tip-Top Towers, the tallest building in town.

"It's Will the window cleaner!" cried Polly Postlady, who had just finished delivering the day's post to the building. "His ladder has broken, and he's hurt his leg. Now he's stuck, and he can't get down! Can you help him?"

"Certainly!" said Fireman Fred. "I can be up there in no time!"

The firemen put up their tallest ladder. While Mike and Dan held out a net – just in case – Fred fearlessly began scrambling up the ladder. "Here I come, Will!" he shouted.

"I've got you!" said Fred, as he grabbed hold of the window cleaner. The crowd below cheered as Fred carried Will down the ladder and helped him into the fire engine.

Fred drove the fire engine straight to the hospital.

"Thank you for rescuing me," Will said to Fred.

"Don't mention it," said Fred. "I'm sure your leg will be fine – but I think you'll need a new ladder!"

"What a busy day it's been!" said Fireman Fred, as they drove back to the fire station. "I feel really frazzled!"

"Our work's not over yet!" said Fireman Dan. "Look! There's smoke up ahead! NEE-NAW! NEE-NAW! went the siren.

VRROOOM! VRROOOM! went the engine, as it raced to the scene of the fire.

The smoke was coming from the fire station! Dan and Mike unwound the hose, and Fred raced inside. "Oooof!" he gasped, as he tripped over the hose and bumped into Benny – again!

"Sorry, fellows," said a red-faced Builder Benny. "I guess I burnt the sausages. I think your lunch is ruined."

Poor Fred felt really frazzled now – until he had an idea. "I know just the person to rescue us from this situation!" he said.

"Who?" asked the others. "Tony!" said Fireman Fred.

"His pizzas are yummy, and an extra-large one will be a perfect lunch for all of us!"

The Smiley Crocodile

Open-wide was the friendliest crocodile for miles around. While all the grumpy crocodiles were snapping and snarling and being very cross, Open-wide grinned at everyone. He had a very, very big smile.

"You smile too much," the others told him. "Be fierce... like a real crocodile!"

"I'll try," said Open-wide, and he put on a scowly face. It lasted two seconds and then the smile came back again. "How was that?" he asked. "Hopeless!" the others said.

One day, some hippos came to the river. They were very large and there were a lot of them. They waded into the part of the river that the crocodiles liked the best. Open-wide liked watching them having fun. He liked it when they sank to the bottom and then came up very slowly making lots of ripples. He liked it when they had a contest to see who could make the biggest splash. He liked it when they blew fountains of water up into the air. The grumpy crocodiles didn't like it one little bit!

"We'll soon get rid of them," they said. Open-wide saw a baby hippo playing in the water. His name was Sausage.

"I bet you can't do this!" said Sausage to Open-wide, and he blew a million bubbles so that they floated in a cloud across the top of the water.

"I bet I can," said Open-wide. And he did... through his nose!

"What about this?" said Sausage, and he turned on his back and sank below the surface. Open-wide did the same, and then he swam very fast to the opposite bank of the river. They played like this all day… and every day after that! Open-wide had never had such a good time.

The grumpy crocodiles were very fed up. They got together to think of ways of getting rid of the hippos. First they tried being frightening by showing lots of teeth. The hippos just smiled… and showed even bigger teeth! Then the grumpy crocodiles tried being rude.

"Scram!" they shouted… and, when that didn't work, "Smelly old hippos!" The hippos thought it was a joke.

Next they charged the hippos while they were swimming. The hippos sank to the bottom of the river where it was too deep for the crocodiles.

The crocodiles didn't know what else to do. Open-wide had an idea! "Why don't I just smile at them and ask nicely if they will move?" he said.

"Pooh!" said the crocodiles. "Fat lot of good that will do!"

Open-wide didn't give up. "Please?" "Oh, go on then," said the grumpy crocodiles, "but it won't work, you'll see."

But it did! The hippos liked Open-wide; he had a big smile just like them. They listened politely when he explained that the crocodiles didn't really like fun. They would rather be on their own and grumpy.

"We'll move further down the river if you will still come and play with Sausage," they said. And that's what happened.

The crocodiles were amazed! They didn't say anything to Open-wide, but secretly they wondered if smiling was better than scowling after all!

Hark the Robbers

Hark at the robbers going through,
 Through, through, through;
  through, through, through;
Hark at the robbers going through,
 My fair lady.

What have the robbers done to you,
 You, you, you; you, you, you?
What have the robbers done to you,
 My fair lady?

Stole my gold watch and chain,
 Chain, chain, chain; chain,
  chain, chain;
Stole my gold watch and chain,
 My fair lady.

How many pounds will set us free,
 Free, free, free; free, free, free?
How many pounds will set us free,
 My fair lady?

A hundred pounds will set you free,
 Free, free, free; free, free, free;
A hundred pounds will set you free,
 My fair lady.

Handy Spandy, Jack-a-Dandy

Handy Spandy, Jack-a-Dandy
 Loved plum-cake and sugar-candy;
He bought some at a grocer's shop,
 And out he came, hop, hop, hop.

There Was a Crooked Man

There was a crooked man, and he went a crooked mile,
 He found a crooked sixpence against a crooked stile;
He bought a crooked cat, which caught a crooked mouse,
 And they all lived together in a little crooked house.

My Father he Died

My father he died, but I can't tell you how,
　　He left me six horses to drive in my plough:
With my wing wang waddle oh,
　　Jack sing saddle oh,
Blowsey boys bubble oh,
　　Under the broom.

I sold my six horses and I bought me a cow,
　　I'd fain have made a fortune
　　　　but did not know how:
With my wing wang waddle oh,
　　Jack sing saddle oh,
Blowsey boys bubble oh,
　　Under the broom.

I sold my cow, and I bought me a calf;
　　I'd fain have made a fortune
　　　　but lost the best half:
With my wing wang waddle oh,
　　Jack sing saddle oh,
Blowsey boys bubble oh,
　　Under the broom.

I Hear Thunder

I hear thunder,
　　I hear thunder,
Oh! don't you?
　　Oh! don't you?

Pitter, patter raindrops,
　　Pitter, patter raindrops,
I'm wet through,
　　I'm wet through.

I see blue skies,
　　I see blue skies,
Way up high,
　　Way up high.

Hurry up the sunshine,
　　Hurry up the sunshine,
I'll soon dry,
　　I'll soon dry.

Three Wise Men of Gotham

Three wise men of Gotham
　　Went to sea in a bowl:
And if the bowl had been stronger,
　　My song would have been longer.

Who Can Save the Chicks?

One morning on Windy Farm, three naughty chicks escaped from their hen house and waddled into the farmyard. "Yippeeeeee!" they cheeped, noisily. "I know that Mummy said we weren't allowed outside the hen house by ourselves," cheeped Chalky Chick, "but there's nothing to do inside! Let's go to the river and play."

"That's a great idea!" cried the other chicks. What fun the chicks had, down by the river. But, as the chicks had fun, they didn't realised that danger was nearby!

Wicked Fox was hiding behind the tree. "Lunch!" he murmured. "I'm going to get them!" Luckily, up in the tree, Owl had woken and spotting Fox he flew off to the farm, for help. But everyone was out searching for the missing chicks. Only Pig was left.

"Quickly," cried Owl to Pig. "Fox is going to eat the chicks!" Pig got up and ran after Owl, as fast as he could. Once Pig got moving, there was no stopping him! And, as he staggered to the river, he crashed into that nasty fox, tossing him into the water with a big, loud SPLASH!

"Everyone was worried about you," said Pig to the little chicks, sternly.

"We're sorry!" cheeped the chicks. "We won't do it again – but getting wet was fun!" And Pig and the chicks dripped all the way back home!

It's Not Fair!

"I want to swim with the ducklings," said Kitten to Mother Cat, as they walked past the pond.

"You can't," Mother Cat told her. "Your fur isn't waterproof."

"I want to roll in the mud with the piglets," said Kitten, when they walked past the pigsty.

"You can't," Mother Cat told her. "Your long fur will get knotted and matted with mud."

"I want to fly with the baby birds," said Kitten to Mother Cat, as she tried to climb where baby birds were learning to fly.

"You can't," Mother Cat told her. "You have fur, not feathers and you haven't got wings. Kittens aren't meant to fly."

"It's not fair!" shouted Kitten. "Kittens don't have any fun!"

Later, Kitten curled up on a rug by the kitchen fire, with a saucer of milk.

"I want to sleep by the fire," said Duckling, standing at the door.

"And I want to lie on a rug," said Piglet, trotting past the door.

"And I want to drink a saucer of milk, said Baby Bird as he flew past.

"It's not fair!" shouted Duckling, Piglet and Baby Bird as Mother Cat shooed them away.

"Oh yes, it is!" mewed Kitten, smiling!

Greedy Bear

If there is one thing in the whole wide world that a teddy bear likes more than anything, it is buns – big sticky currant buns with sugary tops, and squishy middles. A teddy bear will do almost anything for a bun. But for one greedy little teddy bear called Clarence, sticky buns were to be his unsticking!

Rag Doll baked the most wonderful buns in the little toy cooker. She baked big buns and small buns, iced buns and currant buns, Bath buns and cream buns, and even hot cross buns! She shared them out amongst the toys in the playroom, and everybody loved them. But no one loved them as much as Clarence.

"If you will give me your bun, I'll polish your boots!" he'd say to Tin Soldier.

And sometimes, if Tin Soldier was not feeling too hungry, he'd agree. There was always someone who would give Clarence their bun in return for a favour, and sometimes Clarence would eat five or six buns in one day!

Then he'd be busy washing the dolls' dresses, brushing Scotty Dog's fur, or

cleaning the toy policeman's car. He would even stand still and let the clown throw custard pies at him!

So you see, Clarence was not a lazy bear, but he was a greedy bear, and in spite of all his busyness, he was becoming a rather plump little greedy bear. All those buns were starting to show around his middle, and his fur was beginning to strain at the seams!

Then one day Clarence rushed into the playroom full of excitement. His owner, Penny, had told him that next week she was taking him on a teddy bears' picnic.

"She says there will be honey sandwiches and ice cream and biscuits —

and lots and lots of buns!" Clarence told the others, rubbing his paws together. "I can hardly wait! In fact all this excitement has made me hungry, so I think I'll have a bun." And he took a big sticky bun out from under a cushion where he'd hidden it earlier.

"Oh, Clarence!" said Rabbit. "One of these days you will simply go pop!"

"Just be happy I don't like carrots!" said Clarence, with a smile.

Well, that week Clarence was busier than ever. Every time he thought about the picnic he felt hungry, and then he'd have to find someone who'd let him have their bun. He ate bun after bun, and would not listen

when Rag Doll warned him that his back seam was starting to come undone.

The day of the teddy bears' picnic dawned, and Clarence yawned and stretched, smiling with excitement. But as he stretched he felt a popping sensation all down his stomach. He tried to sit up in bed, but to his alarm he found he could not move. He looked down to see that the seams around his tummy had popped open, and his stuffing was spilling out all over the bed!

"Help!" he cried. "I'm exploding!"

Just then, Penny woke up. "Oh, Clarence!" she cried when she saw him. "I can't take you to the teddy bears' picnic like that!"

Penny showed Clarence to her mummy, who said he would have to go to the toy hospital.

Clarence was away from the playroom for a whole week, but when he came back he was as good as new. Some of his stuffing had been taken out, and he was all sewn up again.

He had had lots of time to think in the hospital about what a silly greedy bear he had been. How he wished he had not missed the picnic. The other teddies said it was the best day out they had ever had. Penny had taken Rabbit instead.

"It was terrible," moaned Rabbit. "Not a carrot in sight. I did save you a bun though." And he pulled a big sticky bun out of his pocket.

"No thank you, Rabbit," said Clarence. "I've gone off buns!"

Of course, Clarence did not stop eating buns for long, but from then on he stuck to one a day. And he still did favours for the others, only now he did them for free!

The Chicklings

Duck and Hen both laid some eggs. They were very proud mothers. They would sit with silly smiles on their faces, fondly waiting for their eggs to hatch.

"Duck," said Hen, "let us put the eggs side by side, and see whose eggs are the most beautiful."

"If you like," said Duck, "but I already know mine are."

"Ha!" said Hen. "Wait until you have seen mine!"

Duck carried her eggs carefully, one by one, to a spot where there was soft hay on the ground. Hen carried her eggs over to the same spot and gently put them beside Duck's. Duck picked up the first egg from her side.

"Look at this one! This egg is so smooth!" she said. They both looked at how smooth the egg was. Hen picked up an egg too.

"This one is smooth as well… and it is so round! Look at the lovely shape of this egg." They both looked at the shape of the egg. They put back those two eggs and picked up two others.

Duck said, "This one is smooth and shapely, and has beautiful freckles."

By the time the last one was picked up and put back, the eggs were all mixed up together!

Hen said, "I am fatter than you, so my eggs must be the largest ones."

So Duck picked out the smallest eggs and put them back in her nest. Hen picked out the largest eggs and took them back to hers. Then they sat on them until the eggs hatched and out popped fluffy ducklings and chicks.

One day, Duck and Hen met with their babies.

"Now!" said Duck proudly. "Aren't these the handsomest ducklings you ever saw?"

"They are quite handsome," replied Hen, "but don't you think these are the most beautiful chicks in the whole world?"

"They are quite beautiful," replied Duck.

The next day, Duck taught her ducklings how to be ducklings.

"Walk behind me, one behind the other!" she told them. "We are going to the pond for swimming lessons." But the ducklings just couldn't walk in single file. They ran circles around Duck. They ran over her and under her, until Duck became quite dizzy watching them. At the pond, the ducklings dipped their feet in the water, shook their heads and refused to go in!

Hen was teaching her chicks how to be chicks. She taught them to scratch and hop backwards to make the worms pop up out of the ground. But the chicks couldn't do it! They fell on their faces instead. They just followed her everywhere in a long line.

Duck and Hen knew by now that they had each taken the wrong eggs. The ducklings were chicks, and the chicks were ducklings.

"Never mind," said Hen. "Let's just call them Chicklings, and we will always be right."

And the duck chicklings played happily in the dog's bowl... and the chick chicklings played *on* the dog!

Hippo's Holiday

It was a warm, sunny morning in the jungle.
"A perfect time for a long, relaxing wallow," thought Howard Hippo.
Wallowing in the river was Howard's favourite thing to do. He found a
nice, cool, muddy spot and settled in. Howard was just drifting off into a
delightful daydream, when… SPLASH! "Gotcha!" shrieked Maxine
Monkey. SPLOOSH! "Gotcha back!" shouted Chico Chimp.

"Can't you monkeys and chimps play somewhere else?" Howard
grumbled. "I'm wallowing here!"

"Oops! Sorry, Howard," Maxine apologised. But it was too late.
Howard's wallow was ruined. That afternoon, as the hot sun beat down
on his back, Howard slithered into the river to cool off.

"Aaah," he breathed, as he soaked in the cool water. "This is sooo lovely."

"Yoo-hoo! Howard!" called Penelope Parrot. "I've just learned to do a
double-rollover-loop-the-loop! Want to see?"

"Sure, Penelope," sighed Howard. It didn't look as if he was going to
have a chance to relax this afternoon, either! The next morning, Howard's
cousin, Hilary, came to visit.

"You look exhausted, Howard," she said.

"That's because I never have a chance to relax and wallow any more,"
said Howard.

"What you need is a holiday," said Hilary. "I'm leaving for Hippo

Hollow this afternoon. Why don't you come with me?"

"That sounds like a good idea!" said Howard.

"You'll love Hippo Hollow," said Hilary, as the two hippos trundled through the jungle. "There's so much mud!"

Howard saw himself relaxing in a cool mud bath.

"And there are streams and waterfalls!"continued Hilary. Howard imagined having lots of cool showers.

"And everyone has lots and lots of FUN!" finished Hilary.

Howard thought about playing games with new hippo friends.

At last Howard and Hilary arrived at Hippo Hollow. "It's even more beautiful than I had imagined!" Howard exclaimed.

"And it looks like we've arrived just in time!" said Hilary.

"For what?" asked Howard. "A relaxing mud bath?" "No, silly!" laughed Hilary. "Hippo-robics!"

"Let's get moving, everyone!" called a sleek-looking hippo. Lots of other hippos galloped into the stream behind her.

"Come on, Howard," said Hilary. "Don't be a party pooper on the first day of your holiday!"

Howard had no choice but to join in. "Kick, two, three, four! Kick, two, three, four!" shouted the instructor.

Howard did his best and kicked with all the others. "Surely everyone will want a nice, long rest after all this exercise?" he thought. But he was wrong! After a quick shower in the waterfall, everyone rushed off to play Volley-Melon and Hilary wanted Howard on her team. Howard finally did get to have a rest after lunch — but not for long! "You're looking much more relaxed, Howard," Hilary called, as she led her junior swimming class right past him. "This holiday was just what you needed, wasn't it?"

"Er… I guess so," Howard replied, weakly. After his busy day, Howard was hoping for an early night. He was just getting settled, when he heard Hilary.

"Come on, Howard!" she bellowed. "You don't want to miss the Hippo-Hooray Cabaret! They are really good!"

"Oh — YAWN — how wonderful," sighed Howard. He could barely keep his eyes open.

The next morning, Howard was sliding into the river, when he heard Hilary calling.

"Is it time for Hippo-robics?" he asked.

"Oh, no," said Hilary. "Lots of good, fresh air is what you need. So we're going on a hike!" Howard huffed and puffed all through the exhausting hike. "I hope I can have a nice cool bath when this is over," he thought. Howard got his wish. But, as he was soaking his sore muscles, Hilary came by for a chat.

"The hike was fun, wasn't it?" she said.

"Oh yes," said Howard. "In fact, I enjoyed it so much, that I've decided to go on another one!"

"Really?" said Hilary. "That's great! Where are you hiking to?"

"Home!" said Howard. "I'm going home, where I can have a REAL holiday. And where there are no Hippo-robics, and no Volley-Melon games, no cabarets and no one to stop me wallowing as long as I like!" And so that's exactly what Howard did!

The Spooks' Ball

It is midnight and the spooks are going to the Annual Ball in the old Haunted Hall. By the light of the moon they will dance to a band that will play terrible tunes all night.

A spooks' band has instruments the like of which you will never have seen! The drums are made from skulls of all different shapes and sizes, the piano is made from the teeth of a dinosaur, and the violin is played with a bow made from cats' whiskers. But the strangest sound comes from the skeletons when they take to the dance floor. They shake their bones in time to the band, making a rattling tune which makes them howl with glee! In amongst the shaking skeletons is a witch dancing with her cat, but her boots are so big that she can't keep up with everyone else! A ghost with his head tucked underneath his arm is slowly feeding himself crisps.

As the sun rises the spooks all fade away and the Ball is over for another year – or have you been dreaming?

The Haunted House

Have you ever been in a haunted house? No? Well, follow me and I will take you on a guided tour…

Step carefully through the rusty gates, but be quiet as a mouse, you don't want to upset the residents. Open the front door very slowly – otherwise it will creak and squeak, then everyone will know we are here. The hallway is full of ghosts wafting backwards and forwards, and look… some are walking through the doors when they are closed!

There are ghastly ghouls lurking on the stairs, and imps and sprites are having pillow fights. Look out – you will get covered in feathers!

Push open the kitchen door and a wizard is making slug and spider pies. I don't think we will stay to sample those when they are ready to come out of the oven!

Upstairs, skeletons are getting dressed and vampires are brushing their teeth. A suit of armour is about to get in the bath – we won't stay in case he goes rusty!

So, an ordinary day in a haunted house – would you like to move in?

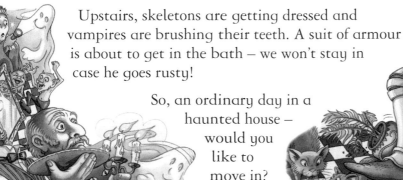

I Saw a Slippery, Slithery Snake

I saw a slippery, slithery snake
   Slide through the grasses,
   Making them shake.
He looked at me with his beady eye.
   "Go away from my pretty green garden," said I.
"Sssss," said the slippery, slithery snake,
   As he slid through the grasses,
   Making them shake.

Round About There

Round about there,
   Sat a little hare,
A cat came and chased him,
   Right up there!

Foxy's Hole

Put your finger in
   Foxy's hole.
   Foxy's not at home.
Foxy's out at the
   back door
   A-picking at a bone

Leg Over Leg

Leg over leg,
   As the dog went to Dover;
When he came to a stile,
   Jump he went over.

Head, Shoulders, Knees and Toes

Head, shoulders, knees and toes, knees and toes,
   Head, shoulders, knees and toes, knees and toes,
And eyes and ears and mouth and nose.
   Head, shoulders, knees and toes, knees and toes.

Clap, Clap Hands

Clap, clap hands, one, two, three,
Put your hands upon your knees,
Lift them up high to touch the sky,
Clap, clap hands and away they fly.

Shoes

Baby's shoes,

Mother's shoes,

Father's shoes,

Policeman's shoes,

GIANT'S SHOES

Tommy Trot

Tommy Trot, a man of law,
Sold his bed and lay upon straw:
Sold the straw and slept on grass,
To buy his wife a looking-glass.

Tall Shop

Tall shop in the town.
Lifts moving up and down.
Doors swinging round about.
People moving in and out.

Five Little Soldiers

Five little soldiers standing in a row,
Three stood straight,
And two stood – so.
Along came the captain,
And what do you think?
They ALL stood straight,
As quick as a wink.

141

Hooray for Pepper!

Pepper was a very noisy puppy. He wasn't a bad puppy. He was just so happy that he barked all day long.

"Woof! Woof!" he barked at the cat, and she hissed and ran away.

"Woof! Woof!" he barked at the birds, and they flew up into the tree.

"Woof! Woof!" he barked at the tree, and it waved its branches angrily.

"Woof! Woof!" he barked at the postman, down the garden path.

"Quiet, Pepper!" shouted Jimmy, Pepper's little boy. But Pepper just barked back cheerfully.

One day, Pepper had been barking so much that everyone was trying very hard to ignore him.

"Be quiet, Pepper," said Jimmy, as he lay down on the lawn. "I'm going to read my book and I can't concentrate if you keep barking."

Pepper tried his very best not to bark. He tried not to watch the butterflies and bees flitting about the garden. He tried to ignore the bright yellow ball lying on the path. And he tried extra hard not to bark at the birds flying high up in the sky. But, everywhere he looked, there were things to bark at, so he decided to stare at the blades of grass on the lawn instead.

As he stared at the grass, Pepper was sure that it began to move. And as he carried on staring, Pepper was sure he could hear a strange slithering sound. He was just about to bark when he remembered Jimmy's words. He carried on staring. Now he could hear a hissing sound. Pepper stared more closely at the grass.

Pepper suddenly started to bark wildly.

"Woof! Woof!" he barked at the grass.

"Sshhh!" groaned Jimmy, as he turned the page of his book.

But Pepper didn't stop. He had spotted something long and slippery slithering across the lawn – something with a long tongue that hissed – and it was heading straight for Jimmy.

"Woof! Woof! WOOF!" barked Pepper.

"Quiet, Pepper!" called Jimmy's dad from the house.

But Pepper did not stop barking. Jimmy sat up, and looked around.

"Snake!" yelled Jimmy, pointing at the long slippery snake coming towards him.

Pepper carried on barking as Jimmy's dad raced across the lawn and scooped Jimmy up in his arms.

Later, after the man from the animal rescue centre had taken the snake away, Jimmy patted Pepper and gave him an extra special doggy treat.

"Hooray for Pepper!" laughed Jimmy. "Your barking really saved the day." That night, Pepper was even allowed to sleep on Jimmy's bed.

And, from that day on, Pepper decided that it was best if he kept his bark for special occasions!

Buried Treasure

Jim lived in a big old house with a big rambling garden. The house was rather spooky, and Jim much preferred the garden. He would spend hours kicking a football around the overgrown lawn, climbing the old apple trees in the orchard or just staring into the pond in case he might spot a fish. It was a wonderful garden to play in, but Jim was not really a happy child because he was lonely. How he wished he had someone to play with! It would be such fun to play football with a friend, or have someone to go fishing with. He had plenty of friends at school, but it was a long bus journey to his home and, besides, his school friends found his house so spooky that they only came to visit once.

One day Jim was hunting about in the garden with a stick. He hoped he might find some interesting small creatures to examine. Every time he found a new creature he would draw it and try to find out its name. So far, he had discovered eight types of snail and six different ladybirds. As he was poking about under some leaves he saw a piece of metal sticking out of the ground.

He reached down and managed to pull it free. In his hand lay a rusty old key. It was quite big, and, as Jim brushed away the soil, he saw that it was carved with beautiful patterns.

Jim carried the key indoors and cleaned it and polished it. Then he set about trying to find the lock that it fitted. First he tried the old garden gate that had been locked as long as Jim could remember. But the key was far too small. Next he tried the grandfather clock in the hall. But the key did not fit the clock's lock. Then he remembered an old wind-up teddy bear that played the drum. Jim hadn't played with the toy for a long time and he eagerly tried out the key, but this time it was too big.

Then Jim had another idea. "Perhaps the key fits something in the attic," he thought. He was usually too scared to go into the attic on his own because it really was scary. But now he was so determined to find the key's home that he

ran up the stairs boldly and opened the door. The attic was dimly lit, dusty and full of cobwebs. The water pipes hissed and creaked and Jim shivered. He began to look under a few dustsheets and opened some old boxes, but didn't find anything that looked as though it needed a key to unlock it. Then he caught sight of a large book sticking out from one of the shelves. It was one of those sorts of books fitted with a lock. Jim lifted down the book, which was extremely heavy, and put it on the floor.

His fingers trembled as he put the key in the lock. It fitted perfectly! He turned the key and the lock sprang open, releasing a cloud of dust. Jim slowly opened the book and turned the pages.

What a disappointment! The pages were crammed with tiny writing and there were no pictures at all. Jim was about to shut the book when he heard a voice coming from the book! "You have unlocked my secrets," it said. "Step into my pages if you are looking for adventure."

Jim was so curious that he found himself stepping on to the book. As he put his foot on the pages he found himself falling through the book. The next thing he knew he was on the deck of a ship. He looked up and

saw a tattered flag with a skull and crossbones flying from a flagpole. He was on a pirate ship! He looked down and saw that he was dressed like a pirate.

The pirate ship was sailing along nicely, when suddenly Jim saw some dangerous-looking rocks in the water – and they were heading straight for them! Before he could shout, the ship had run aground and all the pirates were jumping overboard and swimming to the shore. Jim swam, too.

The water felt deliciously warm and when he reached the shore he found warm sand between his toes. He couldn't believe it! Here he was on a desert island. The pirates went in all directions, searching for something to make a shelter.

Jim looked, too, and under a rock he found a book. The book looked familiar to Jim. He was sure he'd seen it somewhere before. He was still puzzling over it when one of the pirates came running towards him waving a knife. "You thief, you stole my rubies!" cursed the pirate in a menacing voice. What was Jim to do?

Then he heard a voice call from the book, "Quick! Step back here!"

Without thinking twice, Jim stepped into the book and suddenly he was back in the attic again.

Jim peered closely at the page from which he'd just stepped. "The Pirates and the Stolen Treasure" it said at the top of the page. Jim read the page and found he was reading exactly the adventure he had been in. He turned excitedly to the contents page at the front of the book and read the chapter titles. "Journey to Mars", he read, and "The Castle Under the Sea". Further down it said: "The Magic Car" and "Into the Jungle". Jim was thrilled. He realised that he could open the book at any page and become part of the adventure, and he only had to find the book and step into it to get back to the attic again.

After that, Jim had many, many more adventures. He made lots of friends in the stories and he had some narrow escapes. But he always found the book just in time. Jim was never lonely again.

If You Hold My Hand

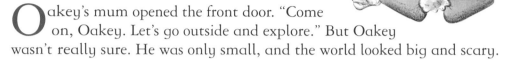

Oakey's mum opened the front door. "Come on, Oakey. Let's go outside and explore." But Oakey wasn't really sure. He was only small, and the world looked big and scary.

"Only if you promise to hold my hand," said Oakey.

So Oakey's mum led him down the long lane. Oakey wished he was back at home again!

"This looks like a great place to play. Shall we take a look? What do you say?" asked Oakey's mum.

"Only if you hold my hand," said Oakey. And Oakey did it!

"Look at me! I can do it!" he cried.

"This slide looks fun. Would you like to try?" asked Oakey's mum.

Oakey looked at the ladder. It stretched right up to the sky.

"I'm only small," said Oakey. "I don't know if I can climb that high – unless you hold my hand." And Oakey did it!

"Wheee! Did you see me?" he cried.

"We'll take a short cut through the wood," said Oakey's mum.

"I'm not sure if we should," said Oakey. "It looks dark in there. Well, I suppose we could – will you hold my hand?" And Oakey did it!

"Boo! I scared you!" he cried.

Deep in the wood, Oakey found a stream, shaded by beautiful tall trees.

"Stepping stones, look!" said Oakey's mum. "Do you think you could jump across these?"

"Maybe," said Oakey. "I just need you to hold my hand, please." And Oakey did it!

One... two... three... four... "Your turn now, Mum," cried Oakey, holding out his hand.

Beyond the wood, Oakey and his mum ran up the hill, and all the way down to the sea. "Come on, Oakey," called his mum. "Would you like to paddle in the sea with me?"

But the sea looked big, and he was only small. Suddenly, Oakey knew that didn't matter at all. He turned to his mum and smiled...

"I can do anything if you hold my hand," he said.

The Golden Bird

There was once a king who kept a golden bird in a gilded cage. The bird wanted for nothing. Every day the king's servant brought him food and water and groomed his fine yellow feathers. And each day the bird sang his beautiful song for the king. "How lucky I am," cried the king, "to have such a beautiful bird that sings such a fine song." However, as time passed the king began to feel sorry for the bird. "It really isn't fair," he thought, "to keep such a handsome creature in a cage. I must give the bird its freedom." He called his servant and ordered him to take the cage into the jungle and release the bird.

The servant obeyed, and took the cage deep into the jungle where he came to a small clearing. He set the cage down, opened the door and out hopped the golden bird. "I hope you can look after yourself," the servant said as he walked away.

The golden bird looked about him. "This is strange!" he thought to himself. "Still, I suppose someone will come along to feed me soon." He settled down and waited.

After a while he heard a crashing sound in the trees, and then he saw a monkey swinging from branch to branch on his long arms.

"Hello there!" called the monkey, hanging by his tail and casting the bird an upside down grin. "Who are you?"

"I am the golden bird," replied the golden bird haughtily.

"I can see you're new around here," said the monkey. "I'll show you the best places to feed in the tree tops."

"No thanks," replied the golden bird ungratefully. "What could an ape like you possibly teach me? You've got such a funny face. I expect you're envious of my beautiful beak," he added.

"Have it your own way," called the monkey as he swung off into the trees.

Some time later the golden bird heard a hissing noise and a snake came slithering by. "Well, hello," hissed the snake. "Who are you?"

"I am the golden bird," replied the golden bird proudly.

"Let me show you the jungle paths," said the snake.

"No thanks," replied the bird rudely. "What could a snake possibly teach me? With your horrid hissing voice, you must be jealous of my beautiful song," he said, forgetting that he had not sung yet.

"Very well," hissed the snake as he slithered and slipped his way into the undergrowth.

By now the golden bird was beginning to wonder when his food would arrive. He began to imagine the tasty morsel that he hoped he would soon be eating.

Just then he was aware of a movement on the tree trunk behind him. Looking up he caught a glimpse of a chameleon, lying camouflaged against the trunk.

"Good day," said the chameleon. "I've been here all the time, so I know who you are. You're the golden bird. It's a good idea to know where to hide in case of danger. Let me show you."

"No thanks," replied the golden bird. "What could an ugly brute like you possibly teach me? You must wish you had lovely feathers like me," he said, fluffing up his beautiful, golden plumage.

"Well, don't say I didn't warn you," muttered the chameleon as he darted away.

The golden bird had just settled down again when a great grey shadow passed over the jungle. He looked up to see a great eagle swooping low over the trees. The monkey swung up to hide in the densest foliage near the top of the trees. The snake slid off to hide in the deepest part of the undergrowth. The chameleon stayed quite still but his skin colour became a perfect match for the tree he was on and he became totally invisible.

"Aha!" thought the golden bird. "All I have to do is fly away and that stupid eagle will never catch up with me." He flapped his wings and flapped and flapped, but he did not know that his wings had grown weak through living a life of luxury in the palace. Now the bird regretted his golden plumage and wished that he had dull brown feathers that would not show up in the forest clearing. For his fine yellow feathers made him easy to see. He was sure the eagle would come and gobble him up. "Help!" he trilled. "Please help me someone." Now he could see the eagle swooping down towards him with eyes blazing like fire and talons drawn.

At that moment the golden bird felt something close around his legs and pull him into the undergrowth. It was the snake. Then he was lifted up into the trees by a long, hairy arm and saw he was being carried by the monkey. "Keep still," whispered the chameleon pushing him into the centre of a large yellow flower. "The eagle won't see you there." And sure enough, the golden bird found that he was precisely the colour of the flower and the eagle flew straight past him.

"How can I repay you all?" exclaimed the bird. "You saved my life!"

"You can sing for us," replied the animals. And so from then on, the monkey, the snake and the chameleon looked after the golden bird, and he sang his beautiful song for them every single day.

The Fluff Monsters

This is the story of the Fluff monsters. Everyone has seen fluff under the bed. That's because the Fluff monsters live under beds.

The Fluff monsters only come out when it's dark. They think it's scary just being out during the day. Who knows what might be out in the daylight? Once, Fluff-boy was having a quiet meal eating fluff and custard, when suddenly the magic-sucking thing appeared. It made a terrible noise as it came closer and closer. Then a tube with a brush on the end sucked up all the fluff after he'd spent ages collecting it!

But Fluff-boy had only ever lived under his bed. He wanted to know what it was like under other beds. "Only naughty Fluff monsters go out in daylight," said Fluff-mummy, "and the Little Girl will get you!"

Fluff-boy's eyes opened wide. "Who's the Little Girl?" he asked.

"The Little Girl is a monster who lives in the bed!" said Fluff-mummy. "She is really clean and pretty! She will take you away and wash you and put you in a room with sun shining through the windows! She will open the doors and fill the room with fresh air from outside!"

"That's horrible! I don't believe you," said Fluff-boy.

"You'll have to be good," said Fluff-mummy, "or you'll find out!"

Well, I'm not scared of the Little Girl!" said Fluff-boy.

Fluff-boy wanted to know what it was like under other beds. One day, while everyone was asleep, Fluff-boy slipped away. Outside, bright sunlight filled the room. He wandered into the next room and found another bed to slide under. There were spiders and daddy-long-legs, cobwebs and lots and lots of fluff! It was perfect! So Fluff-boy ate some fluff (though he did miss his mum's home-made custard) and settled into his new home.

But Fluff-boy couldn't sleep, he was thinking about the Little Girl. Plucking up courage, he carefully climbed up the bed covers. Suddenly, the Little Girl woke and sat up. Fluff-boy was so surprised he jumped with fright. "Aaargh!" shrieked Fluff-boy.

"Aaargh!" screamed the Little Girl. They scrambled to each end of the bed and stared at each other.

"You gave me a fright!" said Fluff-boy.

"Me frighten you?" said the Little Girl. "You frightened me!"

"Did I?" said Fluff-boy. "Why?" laughed Fluff-boy. "I'm Fluff-boy. I've just moved in under this bed. Do you live in this bed too?"

"No, silly," said the Little Girl. "I just sleep here at night. I thought scary Bogeymen lived under the bed. But you're not scary at all!"

"How about this then?" asked Fluff-boy. He stuck his thumbs in his ears, wiggled his fingers and poked out his tongue. The girl laughed.

"That's not at all scary!" she said. "This is scary," and she pulled out the corners of her mouth with her fingers and crossed her eyes. And that was how Fluff-boy and the Little Girl discovered that there is nothing scary under the bed or in it!

Intery, Mintery Cutery, Corn

Intery, mintery, cutery, corn,
   Apple seed and apple thorn.
Wire, briar, limber, lock,
   Three geese in a flock.

One flew east and one flew west;
   One flew over the cuckoo's nest.

Once I Saw a Little Bird

Once I saw a little bird
   Come hop, hop, hop;
So I cried, "Little bird,
   Will you stop, stop, stop?"
And was going to the window,
   To say, "How do you do?"
But he shook his little tail,
   And far away he flew.

Little Robin Redbreast

Little Robin Redbreast
   Sat upon a rail:
Niddle-noddle went his head!
   Wiggle-waggle went his tail.

The North Wind Doth Blow

The north wind doth blow,
   And we shall have snow,
And what will poor Robin do then?
   Poor thing!

He'll sit in a barn,
   And to keep himself warm,
Will hide his head under his wing.
   Poor thing!

While We Were Walking

While we were walking, we were watching window washers wash Washington's windows with warm washing water.

Two Little Dicky Birds

Two little dicky birds sitting on a wall,
One named Peter, one named Paul.
    Fly away, Peter!
    Fly away, Paul!
        Come back, Peter!
        Come back, Paul!

Little Wind

Little wind, blow on the hill-top;
    Little wind, blow down the plain;
Little wind, blow up the sunshine;
    Little wind, blow off the rain.

KATE GREENAWAY

The Cuckoo

Cuckoo, Cuckoo,
    What do you do?
In April
    I open my bill;
In May
    I sing night and day;
In June
    I change my tune;
In July
    Away I fly;
In August
    Away I must.

Magpies

One for sorrow, two for joy,
    Three for a girl, four for a boy,
Five for silver, six for gold,
    Seven for a secret never to be told.

Jay-bird

Jay-bird, jay-bird, settin' on a rail,
    Pickin' his teeth with the end of his tail;
Mulberry leaves and calico sleeves —
    All school teachers are hard to please.

Crocodile Smiles

"Say cheese!" said the photographer.
"CHEESE!" grinned Snappy, the crocodile. Lights flashed, and cameras clicked as he gave his most winning smile.

"You're a natural!" cried the expedition leader. He was with a team of wildlife photographers. Snappy smiled at his reflection in the river.

"Ooh, you are a handsome chap!" he preened, gnashing his fine set of teeth together with glee.

Snappy was terribly proud of his sharp fangs, and fine good looks. He strutted up and down the river bank for all to see.

"I'm a star!" he said. "My face will be known throughout the world!"

"Thanks for letting us take your picture," said the expedition leader.

"No problem," said Snappy. "Any time!"

"And, as your reward, here's the truck load of chocolate you asked for," said the leader.

"How delicious!" said Snappy. "Most kind of you. Thank you so much."

When they had gone, Snappy lay sunning himself on the river bank, daydreaming of fame and fortune, and popping chocolate after chocolate into his big, open mouth.

Just then, along slithered Snake.

"What's thissss?" he hissed. "A crocodile eating chocolate? How very ssssstrange!"

"Not at all!" snapped Snappy. "All crocodiles love chocolate. It's just that most of them aren't clever enough to know how to get hold of it."

"Well, if you're so sssmart, you ssshould know that too much chocolate will make your teeth fall out!" hissed Snake.

"What rot!" said Snappy, crossly. "For your information, I've got perfect teeth."

"Lucky you!" said Snake, and slithered off into the bushes.

So Snappy carried on munching happily, eating his way through the mound of chocolate. He had chocolate for breakfast, chocolate for lunch and chocolate for dinner.

"Ooh, yummy!" he grinned, licking his lips and smiling a big, chocolatey smile. "This is heaven."

"You won't be saying that when you are too fat to float in the river," said Parrot, who had been watching him from a tree.

"Nonsense!" scoffed Snappy. "I've got a very fine figure, I'll have you know!"

"If you say so," said Parrot, and flew off into the jungle.

Days and weeks passed, and Snappy happily carried on eating chocolate after chocolate, until at last it was all gone.

"Back to the river to catch my next meal, then," Snappy thought miserably. "Though I'd much rather have more chocolate!"

But, when Snappy slid into the river, instead of bobbing gently at the surface, he sank straight to the bottom, and his stomach rested in the mud.

"Oh dear, what's happened to the river?" Snappy wondered aloud to himself. "It's very hard to float in today."

"Even for someone with such a fine figure as you?" jeered Parrot, watching from the trees. Snappy didn't answer. He just sank further beneath the water so that only his two beady eyes could be seen, and gave Parrot a very hard stare.

The next morning when he awoke there was a terrible pain in his mouth. It felt like someone was twisting and tugging on his teeth. "Oww, my teeth hurt!" he cried.

"Sssurely not!" hissed Snake, dangling down from a tree. "After all, you have sssuch perfect teeth!" and he slunk away again, snickering.

Snappy knew what he had to do. He set off down the river to visit **Mr Drill** the dentist.

It seemed such a long, hard walk, and by the time he got there he was puffing and panting.

"Open wide!" said Mr Drill, an anteater, peering down his long nose into Snappy's gaping mouth. "Oh dear. This doesn't look good at all. What have you been eating, Snappy? Now show me where it hurts."

"Here," said Snappy pointing miserably into his mouth, and feeling rather ashamed, "and here, and here, and here..."

"Well, there's nothing for it," said Mr Drill, "they'll have to come out!" And so out they came!

Before long, another photography expedition arrived in the jungle.

"Say cheese!" said the expedition leader.

"CHEESE!" smiled Snappy, stepping out from behind a tree. But, instead of a flash of cameras, Snappy met with howls of laughter, as the photographers fell about holding their sides.

"I thought you said Snappy was a handsome crocodile with perfect teeth!" they cried, looking at the leader. "He should be called Gappy, not Snappy!"

Poor Snappy slunk away into the bushes and cried. It was all his own fault for being so greedy and eating all that chocolate.

"There, there," said Mr Drill, patting his arm. "We'll soon fit you out with some fine new teeth."

And from then on, Snappy vowed he would never eat chocolate again!

Desmond Grows Up

Desmond was the smallest monkey in the group. He couldn't wait to grow up. "Will you measure me?" he asked his friend Rodney. "I only measured you last Monday, and now it's Friday," said Rodney. "You won't have grown in four days!"

Rodney took him to the tallest tree in the jungle and made him stand with his back against it. Then he made a mark on the trunk at the top of Desmond's head. It was in the same place as the last mark.

"See," he said, "you are still the same size."

"Botheration!" said Desmond.

Later he spoke to his friend Bubbles. "Watch the top of my head," he said to her.

"Whatever for, Dethmond?" said Bubbles. She always called him Dethmond.

"Just watch," said Desmond. So Bubbles watched the top of his head.

"Well?" asked Desmond. "Well what?" replied Bubbles.

"Am I growing? Can you see me growing?" asked Desmond.

"No, of course not!" she said. "I knew it!" said Desmond. "I knew it! I'm never going to grow."

"Dethmond," said Bubbles, "you will grow! Honestly you will."

But Desmond was not so sure. "What can I do to get taller?" he asked Rodney. "Wait!" said Rodney. So Desmond stood next to Rodney... and waited. And waited. "You won't grow that fast!" laughed Rodney. "It will be ages before you grow up."

But Desmond didn't have ages. He wanted to collect coconuts... NOW! He tried to stretch. He asked all his friends to pull on his arms and legs and to squeeze him so that he would get thinner and taller. He hung from the branches of trees by his toes. Nothing worked!

Every day he watched as the other monkeys climbed the tall palm trees to pick coconuts and drop them to the ground.

One day, there was a competition to see who could collect the most coconuts. Rodney was the favourite to win. He climbed to the top and wriggled through the palm leaves, and then... oh dear... he got stuck!

"Help!" he called." I can't move." One of the other big monkeys went up to help, but he was too big to get through the leaves.

"Let me try," begged Desmond.

"OK," they said grudgingly. Desmond raced up the trunk. At the top he was small enough to reach his friend and help him to get free. Then he picked six or seven coconuts and dropped them to the ground.

When they climbed down the other monkeys crowded round to pat Desmond on the back.

"Wow!" said Bubbles. "No one has ever climbed a tree that fast before."

"Maybe you are all too big!" said Desmond happily. "I'm not in such a hurry to grow up after all!"

After that he didn't worry so much about being small, especially after he managed to collect more coconuts than anyone else, and won the competition!

Mr Squirrel Won't Sleep

It was autumn. The leaves were falling from the trees in the forest and the air was cold. All the animals began to get ready for winter.

One night Mr Fox came back from hunting and said to his wife, "There's not much food about now it's getting colder. We'd better start storing what we can to help tide us over the winter."

"You're right, Mr Fox," replied his wife, gathering her cubs into their lair.

"I'd love to go fishing," said Mr Bear, "but I'll have to wait until spring now." He went into his den, shut the door tight and sealed it.

Mrs Mouse ran by with a mouthful of straw. "Must dash," she squeaked, "or my winter bed will never be finished in time." But soon she, too, was curled up with her tail wrapped around her for warmth.

Now only Mr Squirrel wasn't ready for winter. He danced about in his tree, leaping from branch to branch and chasing his tail. "Ha, ha!" he boasted. "I don't have to get ready for winter. I have a fine store of nuts hidden away, a beautiful bushy tail to keep me warm and, besides, I don't feel in the least bit sleepy." And he carried on playing in his tree.

"Are you still awake?" snapped Mr Fox.

"Go to sleep!" growled Mr Bear.

"Please be quiet," squeaked Mrs Mouse, drawing her tail more tightly about her ears.

But Mr Squirrel wouldn't go to sleep. He danced up and down all the more and shouted, "I'm having SUCH FUN!" at the top of his voice.

Winter came. The wind whistled in the trees' bare branches, the sky turned grey and it became bitterly cold. Then it started to snow. At first Mr Squirrel had a grand time making snowballs – but there was no one around to throw them at and he began to feel rather lonely. Soon he felt cold and hungry, too.

"No problem!" he said to himself. "I'll have some nice nuts to eat. Now, where did I bury them?" He scampered down his tree to find that the ground was deep with snow. He ran this way and that trying to find his hiding places, but all the forest looked the same in the snow and soon he was hopelessly lost.

"Whatever shall I do?" he whimpered, for now he was shivering with cold and hunger and his beautiful, bushy tail was all wet and bedraggled.

All of a sudden he thought he heard a small voice. But where was it coming from? He looked all around but there was no sign of anyone.
Then he realised that the voice was coming from under the snow.

"Hurry up!" said the voice. "You can join me down here, but you'll have to dig a path to my door."

Mr Squirrel started digging with his front paws and sure enough there was a path leading to a door under a tree stump. The door was just open enough for Mr Squirrel to squeeze his thin, tired body through.

Inside was a cosy room with a huge fire, and sitting by the fire was a tiny elf. "I heard you running around up there and thought you might be in need of a bit of shelter," said the elf. "Come and sit by the fire." Mr Squirrel was only too pleased to accept and soon he was feeling warm and dry.

"This isn't my house, you know," said the elf. "I think it might be part of an old badgers' sett. I got lost in the forest and so, when I found this place, I decided to stay here until spring. Though how I'll ever find my way home, I don't know." A fat tear rolled down the elf's cheek.

"I have been a very foolish squirrel," said Mr Squirrel. "If you hadn't taken me in I surely would have died. I am indebted to you and, if you will let me stay here until spring, I will help you find your way home."

"Please stay!" replied the elf. "I'd be glad of the company." So Mr Squirrel settled down with his tail as a blanket and soon he was asleep.

Days and nights passed, until one day the elf popped his head out of the door and exclaimed, "The snow has melted, spring is coming. Wake up, Mr Squirrel." Mr Squirrel rubbed his eyes and looked out. There were patches of blue in the sky and he could hear a bird singing.

"Climb on my back," Mr Squirrel said. "I'll show you the world."

They set off through the forest until they climbed to the top of the highest tree of all.

"You can look now," said Mr Squirrel, seeing that the elf had covered his eyes with his tiny hands. The elf had never seen anything like it in his whole life. Stretching in all directions, as far as the eye could see, were mountains, lakes, rivers, forests and fields. Suddenly the elf started to jump for joy.

"What is it?" said Mr Squirrel.

"I... I... can see my home," cried the elf, pointing down into the valley below the forest. "And there are my friends sitting in the sunshine. I must go home, Mr Squirrel. Thank you for showing me the world, for I should never have seen my home again without you." And with that he climbed down the tree and skipped all the way home.

Mr Squirrel made his way back to his own tree where Mrs Mouse, Mr Fox and Mr Bear were very pleased to see him.

"I've been very foolish, but I've learned my lesson," said Mr Squirrel. "Now let's have a party – I've got rather a lot of nuts to eat up!"

So the animals celebrated spring with a fine feast. And Mr Squirrel vowed not to be silly again next winter.

Danny Duckling in Trouble

"Stay still so I can count!" quacked Mummy Duck crossly, as the little ducklings splashed about. "Just as I thought, Danny's missing again. We'd better go and look for him!" It was the third time that week Danny Duckling had got lost. He liked to swim at the end of the line and often got left behind. But this time he was in trouble…

Earlier that day, Danny had been following along through the reeds when his foot caught in something beneath the water.

"Bother!" he quacked as he tried to pull it free. He ducked into the water and saw that his foot was tangled in an old fishing net held fast in the mud. "Help!" he cried to the others, but they were already too far away to hear. The more Danny struggled, the tighter the net gripped his foot. "Help!" he quacked, flapping his fluffy little wings.

Luckily, Freya Frog heard his cries and dived under the water to try and free him, but it was no use. "I'll go and get help," she said, swimming off.

"Hurry!" Danny called after her. The tide was coming in and the river was rising fast!

By the time Freya returned with Wally Water Rat, the water was covering Danny's back. "I'm going to be pulled under!" cried Danny. "Don't worry," said Wally. "We'll save you!" In no time at all, Wally's sharp teeth nibbled through the net, and Danny bobbed back to the surface just as his Mummy appeared.

"Thank goodness you're safe," said Mummy. "But from now on swim at the front of the line." And that is just what Danny did.

Oh Dear, What Can the Matter Be?

Oh dear, what can the matter be?
  Dear, dear, what can the matter be?
Oh dear, what can the matter be?
  Johnny's so long at the fair.

He promised he'd buy me a basket of posies,
  A garland of lilies, a garland of roses,
A little straw hat to set off the blue ribbons
  That tie up my bonny brown hair.

Oh dear, what can the matter be?
  Dear, dear, what can the matter be?
Oh dear, what can the matter be?
  Johnny's so long at the fair.

Goosey Goosey Gander

Goosey, goosey, gander,
  Whither shall I wander?
Upstairs and downstairs,
  And in my lady's chamber.
There I met an old man
  Who would not say his prayers
I took him by the left leg
  And threw him down the stairs

Knick Knack Paddy Whack

This old man, he played one,
  He played knick knack on my drum.
With a knick knack paddy whack, give a dog a bone,
  This old man went rolling home.

This old man, he played two,
  He played knick knack on my shoe.
With a knick knack paddy whack, give a dog a bone,
  This old man went rolling home.

Jack and Jill

Jack and Jill went up the hill
    To fetch a pail of water;
Jack fell down and broke his crown
    And Jill came tumbling after.

Up Jack got and home did trot
    As fast as he could caper;
He went to bed to mend his head
    With vinegar and brown paper.

Cock-a-Doodle-Doo

Cock-a-doodle-doo!
    My dame has lost her shoe,
My master's lost his fiddling stick,
    And doesn't know what to do.

Cock-a-doodle-doo!
    What is my dame to do?
Till master finds his fiddling stick,
    She'll dance without her shoe.

Cock-a-doodle-doo!
    My dame has found her shoe,
And master's found his fiddling stick,
    Sing cock-a-doodle-doo!

Girls and Boys Come Out to Play

Girls and boys, come out to play;
    The moon doth shine as bright as day;
Leave your supper, and leave your sleep,
    And come with your playfellows into the street.

Come with a whoop, come with a call,
    Come with a good will or not at all.
Up the ladder and down the wall,
    A halfpenny roll will serve us all.
You find milk, and I'll find flour,
    And we'll have a pudding in half an hour.

Little Tim and his Brother Sam

Little Tim was a very lucky boy. He had a lovely home, with the nicest parents you could hope for. He had a big garden, with a swing and a football net in it. And growing in the garden were lots of trees that you could climb and have adventures in. Little Tim even had a nice school, which he enjoyed going to every day and where he had lots of friends. In fact, almost everything in Tim's life was nice. Everything that is apart from one thing – Tim's brother Sam.

Sam was a very naughty boy. Worse still, whenever he got into mischief – which he did almost all of the time – he managed to make it look as though someone else was to blame. And that someone was usually poor Tim!

Once Sam thought that he would put salt in the sugar bowl instead of sugar. That afternoon, Sam and Tim's parents had some friends round for tea. All the guests put salt in their cups of tea, of course, thinking it was sugar. Well, being very polite they didn't like to complain,

even though their cups of tea tasted *very* strange! When Sam and Tim's parents tasted their tea, however, they guessed immediately that someone had been playing a trick. They had to apologise to their guests and make them all fresh cups of tea. And who got the blame? Little Tim did, because Sam had sprinkled salt on Tim's bedroom floor so that their mother would think that Tim was the culprit.

Then there was the time when Sam and Tim's Aunt Jessica came to stay. She was a very nice lady, but she hated anything creepy-crawly, and as far as she was concerned that included frogs. So what did Sam do? Why, he went down to the garden pond and got a big, green frog to put in Aunt Jessica's handbag. When Aunt Jessica opened her handbag to get her glasses out, there staring out of the bag at her were two froggy eyes.

"Croak!" said the frog.

"Eeek!" yelled Aunt Jessica and almost jumped out of her skin.

"I told Tim not to do it," said Sam.

Tim opened his mouth and was just about to protest his innocence when his mother said, "Tim, go to your room immediately and don't come out until you are told."

Poor Tim went to his room and had to stay there until after supper. Sam thought it was very funny.

The next day, Sam decided that he would play another prank and blame it on Tim. He went to the garden shed and, one by one, took out all the garden tools. When he thought no one was watching, he hid them all in Tim's bedroom cupboard. In went the spade, the fork, the watering can, the trowel – in fact, everything except the lawnmower. And the only reason that the lawnmower didn't go in was because it was too heavy to carry!

But this time, Sam's little prank was about to come unstuck, for Aunt Jessica had seen him creeping up the stairs to Tim's bedroom with the garden tools. She guessed immediately what Sam was up to, and who was likely to get the blame. When Sam wasn't about, she spoke to Tim. The two of them whispered to each other for a few seconds and then smiled triumphantly.

Later that day, Sam and Tim's father went to the garden shed to fetch the tools to do some gardening. Imagine his surprise when all he saw were some old flower pots and the lawnmower. He searched high and low for the garden tools. He looked behind the compost heap, under the garden steps, behind the sandpit and in the garage. But they weren't anywhere to be seen.

Then he started searching in the house. He looked in all the kitchen cupboards, and was just looking under the

stairs when something at the top of the stairs caught his eye. The handle from the garden spade was sticking out of the door to Sam's bedroom. Looking rather puzzled, he went

upstairs and walked into Sam's bedroom. There, nestling neatly in the cupboard, were the rest of the tools.

"Sam, come up here immediately," called his father.

Sam, not realising anything was amiss, came sauntering upstairs. Suddenly he saw all the garden tools that he had so carefully hidden in Tim's cupboard now sitting in *his* cupboard. He was speechless.

"Right," said his father, "before you go out to play, you can take all the tools back down to the garden shed. Then you can cut the grass. Then you can dig over the flower beds, and then you can do the weeding."

Well, it took Sam hours to do all the gardening. Tim and Aunt Jessica watched from the window and clutched their sides with laughter. Sam never did find out how all the garden tools found their way into his bedroom, but I think you've guessed, haven't you?

Don't Care

Don't-care didn't care;
  Don't-care was wild.
Don't-care stole plum and pear
  Like any beggar's child.
Don't-care was made to care,
  Don't-care was hung:
Don't-care was put in the pot
  And boiled till he was done.

The Oxen

Christmas Eve, and twelve of the clock.
  "Now they are all on their knees,"
An elder said as we sat in a flock
  By the embers in hearthside ease.

We pictured the meek mild
    creatures where
  They dwelt in their strawy pen,
Nor did it occur to one of us there
  To doubt they were kneeling then.

So fair a fancy few would weave
  In these years! Yet, I feel,
If someone said on Christmas Eve,
  "Come; see the oxen kneel

"In the lonely barton by yonder coomb
  Our childhood used to know,"
I should go with him in the gloom,
  Hoping it might be so.

Where Go the Boats?

Dark brown is the river,
  Golden is the sand.
It flows along for ever,
  With trees on either hand.

Green leaves a-floating,
  Castles of the foam,
Boats of mine a-boating –
  Where will all come home?

On goes the river,
  And out past the mill,
Away down the valley,
  Away down the hill.

Away down the river,
  A hundred miles or more,
Other little children
  Shall bring my boats ashore.

ROBERT LOUIS STEVENSON

Eldorado

Gaily bedight
    A gallant knight,
In sunshine and in shadow,
    Had journeyed long,
    Singing a song,
    In search of Eldorado.

But he grew old –
    This knight so bold –
And o'er his heart a shadow
    Fell as he found
No spot of ground
    That looked like Eldorado.

And, as his strength
    Failed him at length,
He met a pilgrim shadow:
    "Shadow," said he,
    "Where can it be,
    This land of Eldorado?"

"Over the mountains
    Of the Moon,
Down the valley of
    the Shadow,
Ride, boldly ride,"
    The shade replied,
"If you seek for Eldorado."

The Mouse's Lullaby

Oh, rock-a-by, baby mouse, rock-a-by, so!
When baby's asleep to the baker's I'll go,
And while he's not looking I'll pop from a hole,
And bring to my baby a fresh penny roll.

The Duel

The gingham dog and the calico cat
    Side by side on the table sat;
'Twas half-past twelve, and
        (what do you think!)
    Nor one nor t'other had slept a wink!
The old Dutch clock and the Chinese plate
    Appeared to know as sure as fate
There was going to be a terrible spat.
(I wasn't there; I simply state
    What was told to me by the Chinese plate!)

The gingham dog went "Bow-wow-wow!"
    And the calico cat replied "mee-ow!"
The air was littered, an hour or so,
    With bits of gingham and calico,
While the old Dutch clock in the
        chimney-place
    Up with its hands before its face,
For it always dreaded a family row!
(Now mind: I'm only telling you
    What the old Dutch clock declares is true!)

I Wish...

I wonder what you would be if you weren't you. I like to sit and think of all the things I would like to be...

Sometimes I wish I was an elephant because it would make me laugh to sit in the bath and use my nose as a hose to rinse off all my bubbles.

Or I wish I was a chameleon because then I could change the colour of my skin to hide anywhere, and no one would be able to see me!

If I was a hippo I would be able to mess about all day and get as dirty as I liked, and no one would tell me off.

Or if I could be a dolphin I would be able to leap and splash about in the water having fun all day, and swim with the fish.

I suppose I could be an ostrich, but I am not sure that if I was frightened I would really want to hide my head in the sand!

I think that I will stay as me – but I won't stop wondering about being something else!

A Whale of a Time

Have you heard the story of Wendy Bligh? She was a remarkable whale who loved to fly!

One day Wendy was sleeping peacefully, bobbing along in the sea, when a hot-air balloonist flew by her. He looked down from his balloon basket and spotted her hump.

"I think I will land on that rock," he said to himself. He tied up his balloon, and all the time Wendy carried on sleeping completely unaware of the balloonist.

But then a tornado whirled over the sea and blew the balloon and Wendy upwards as high as can be.

"What a wonderful feeling" cried Wendy in glee. "I am floating above the sparkling blue sea."

The hot-air balloonist took her for a spin, then dropped her back in the sea at the end of the day.

"Oh thank you!" smiled Wendy and swam away.

Lost for Ever

Sheep are lovely animals, but they are not the cleverest creatures. They follow one another without thinking too much about whether it is a good idea. When the leader is Maria, it very often isn't!

One day, Maria thought that the grass in the next meadow was much greener and juicier than the grass right under her nose.

"Come on, girls!" she baa-ed. "Follow me!"

With a skip and a jump, Maria was over the fence and into the meadow next door, and it wasn't long before the other sheep had followed Maria into the next field, too.

After an hour of munching grass in the new meadow, Maria happened to look over the wall on the far side. The grass there looked even better. "Follow me!" she baa-ed again, and she was off! The other sheep were right behind her.

By the end of the afternoon, Maria and her friends found themselves a very long way from Old MacDonald's farm and seemed likely to be lost for ever!

"I don't know where we are," said Maria, looking all around her. "Oh, I can't think now. I'm going to sleep."

And, of course, all the other sheep were soon asleep, too.

Now, when sheep wake up, they are hungry! So the next morning, when Maria awoke, she forgot about trying to find her way home. Instead, she tucked into some tasty grass.

You can guess what the other sheep did!

Maria grazed her way across the meadow and came to a hedge. Over the hedge was another meadow, and the grass looked even tastier there. "Follow me, girls!" Maria baa-ed. So, with a skip, a jump and a leap, the flock bounded into the meadow and started on their mid-morning snack.

At lunch time, tea time and supper time, exactly the same thing happened.

It wasn't until it was bedtime that Maria remembered that they were a long way from home. "We must be even further now," she baa-ed, sadly.

"But maaamaaa…" bleated her little lamb.

"Tell me in the morning," Maria replied.

"But maaamaaa…" the lamb tried again.

"Go to sleep, little one," said Maria. "We'll get home tomorrow."

"But MAAAMAAA!" laughed the little lamb. "We are home already. Look! What can you see?"

And, sure enough, there before them was Old MacDonald's meadow.

The smoke from the farmhouse chimney drifted into the evening air. Old MacDonald stood by the gate. Without intending to, Maria had led them all the way back home again.

Although sheep are not clever creatures, sometimes they are silly in a very clever way – if you see what I mean!

Bone Crazy

Alfie sat in his basket chewing on a large bone. Mmm! It tasted good. When he had chewed it for long enough, he took it down to the bottom of the garden, to bury it in his favourite spot, beneath the old oak tree. He didn't see next door's dog, Ferdy, watching him through a hole in the fence.

The next day, when Alfie went to dig up his bone, it was gone! He dug all around, but it was nowhere to be found. Just then, he spied a trail of muddy paw prints leading to the fence, and he realised what had happened. Alfie was too big to fit through the fence and get his bone back, so he thought of a plan, instead! Next day he buried another bone. This time, he knew Ferdy was watching him.

Later he hid and watched as Ferdy crept into the garden and started to dig up the bone. Just then, Ferdy yelped in pain. The bone had bitten his nose! He flew across the garden and through the fence leaving the bone behind.

Alfie's friend Mole crept out from where the bone was buried. How the two friends laughed at their trick! And from then on, Ferdy always kept safely to his side of the fence!

Little Jack Jingle

Little Jack Jingle,
   He used to live single:
But when he got tired of this kind of life,
He left off being single, and lived with
   his wife.

Little Tommy Tittlemouse

Little Tommy Tittlemouse
   Lived in a little house;
He caught fishes
   In other men's ditches.

Harry Parry

O rare Harry Parry,
   When will you marry?
When apples and pears are ripe.
I'll come to your wedding,
   Without any bidding,
And dance and sing all the night.

Young Roger Came Tapping

Young Roger came tapping at Dolly's window,
   Thumpaty, thumpaty, thump!
He asked for admittance, she answered him "No!"
   Frumpaty, frumpaty, frump!

"No, no, Roger, no! as you came you may go!"
   Stumpaty, stumpaty, stump!

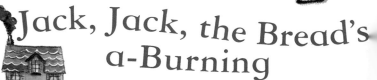

Jack, Jack, the Bread's a-Burning

Jack, Jack, the bread's a-burning,
   All to a cinder;
If you don't come and fetch it out
   We'll throw it through the window.

Robin and Richard

Robin and Richard were two pretty men;
    They laid in bed till the clock struck ten;
Then up starts Robin and looks at the sky,
    Oh! brother Richard, the sun's very high:

The bull's in the barn threshing the corn,
    The cock's on the dunghill blowing his horn,
The cat's at the fire frying of fish,
    The dog's in the pantry breaking his dish.

If a Pig Wore a Wig

If a pig wore a wig,
    What could we say?
Treat him as a gentleman,
    And say "Good-day".

If his tail chanced to fail,
    What could we do?
Send him to the tailoress
    To get one new.

CHRISTINA ROSSETTI

Tom, Tom, the Piper's Son

Tom, Tom, the piper's son,
    Stole a pig, and away he run.
The pig was eat, and Tom was beat,
    And Tom went roaring down the street.

Jack and Guy

Jack and Guy went out in the rye,
    And they found a little boy with one black eye.
Come, says Jack, let's knock him on the head.
    No, says Guy, let's buy him some bread;
You buy one loaf and I'll buy two,
    And we'll bring him up as other folk do.

Bob Robin

Little Bob Robin,
    Where do you live?
Up in yonder wood, sir,
    On a hazel twig.

Milly the Greedy Puppy

Milly the Labrador puppy just loved eating. She wasn't fussy about what she ate, and didn't really mind whom it belonged to.

"You'll get fat," warned Tom, the farm cat. But Milly was too busy chewing a tasty fishbone to take any notice.

One day, Milly was in a particularly greedy mood. Before breakfast she sneaked into the kitchen and ate Tom's biscuits. After a big breakfast of fresh sardines and milk, she took a short break before nibbling her way through the horse's oats. The horse didn't seem to mind.

Then Milly had a quick nap. She felt quite hungry when she awoke, so she ate all the tastiest titbits from the pigs' trough. But she made sure she left plenty of room for lunch.

After a light lunch, Milly couldn't help feeling just a bit hungry – so she wolfed down Farmer Jones's meat pie. He'd left it on the window ledge so he obviously didn't want it.

After that, Milly knocked over the dustbin and rifled through the kitchen waste. It was full of the yummiest leftovers.

There was just enough time for another nap before nipping into the milking shed for milking time. Milly always enjoyed lapping up the odd bucketful of fresh milk when Farmer Jones wasn't looking.

Dinner was Milly's favourite meal of the day. It was amazing how fast she could eat a huge bowl of meat and biscuits.

Before going to bed, Milly walked around the yard cleaning up the scraps the hens had left behind. Wasn't she a helpful puppy!

Just as Milly was chewing a particularly tasty bit of bread, she saw something black out of the corner of her eye. It was Tom the farm cat, out for his evening stroll. If there was one thing Milly liked doing best of all, it was eating Tom's dinner when he wasn't looking.

Milly raced across the yard, around the barn and through the cat flap.

"Woof! Woof!" yelped Milly. She was stuck half-way through the cat flap. Greedy Milly had eaten so much food that her tummy was too big to fit through.

"Ha! Ha!" laughed the farm animals, who thought it served Milly right for eating all their food.

"Oh, dear!" smiled Tom when he came back to see what all the noise was about. He caught hold of Milly's legs and tried pulling her out. Then he tried pushing her out. But it was no good – she was stuck.

All the farm animals joined in. They pulled and pulled, until, POP! Out flew Milly.

Poor Milly felt so silly that she never ate anyone else's food again – unless they offered, that is!

Tractor Trouble

Old MacDonald loves his tractor, but it can be as troublesome as the naughtiest piglet. One cold and frosty morning, it sat in the barn and refused to start.

"I must plough the far field before the new lambs are born," groaned Old MacDonald, "while I still have the time."

But the tractor did not start. It coughed and wheezed, and a few puffs of black smoke came out of the exhaust. But there was none of the roaring noise that Old MacDonald liked to hear.

"I'll just have to call the mechanic," he said crossly, stomping towards the farmhouse.

Unfortunately, the mechanic was busy for the rest of the week.

"Listen carefully while I tell you what to do," he told Old MacDonald helpfully.

So the farmer trudged back to the barn, his head full of thoughts of pipes, plugs and pumps – not at all sure he had understood what the mechanic had said!

But, the moment Old MacDonald opened up the engine's bonnet, he knew exactly what the problem was – and he wasn't angry at all. A little mouse had made her nest there and was busy taking care of six tiny babies!

"Don't worry," whispered Old MacDonald, "I'll find you somewhere better to live."

So Old MacDonald started searching the barn for a special place for the mouse and her family to make their home. It had to be warm and

cosy. It had to be somewhere that Milly and Lazy the cats couldn't reach.

Looking through all the junk and clutter stored in the barn was hot work, so Old MacDonald hung his coat from a beam. By the end of the morning, the barn looked a lot tidier, but he still hadn't found a home for the mouse family.

"Come and have your lunch," called his wife. "And don't even think about bringing those mice into my kitchen!"

But, as Old MacDonald went to take his coat down from the beam, he suddenly had a good idea…

Ten minutes later, the mouse family had a lovely new home, and Old MacDonald was enjoying his lunch at last. All that work to tidy the barn had made him hungry, and he was very pleased to have found a home for the mouse family.

"I'm off to do the ploughing now," he said to his wife when he had finished. "Where is my old jacket?"

Mrs MacDonald looked surprised. "Why?" she began. Then she smiled. "I suppose you've lent your coat to someone else for a while."

Old MacDonald found his old coat and went back to the barn. This time the tractor roared into life.

"A little less noise until we get outside, old friend," smiled Old MacDonald. "We don't want to wake the babies."

The Smart Bear and the Foolish Bear

It was the start of winter. The first snow had fallen, and the lake had begun to freeze. It was nearly time for all the bears to start their winter sleep. But there was one foolish bear who wasn't ready to sleep yet. "I'll just catch one more fish," he told himself, "to keep me going through winter." And, although he knew it was dangerous, he crept out onto the icy lake.

He lay down on his tummy, and broke a hole in the ice. He could see lots of fish swimming in the water below. He dipped his paw into the hole, and scooped out a fish in a flash! But the foolish little bear leapt up, shouting, "I caught one!" With a great crack, the ice gave way beneath him, and he fell into the freezing water!

Luckily a smart little bear cub heard his cries, and rushed to help. He found a fallen log and pushed it over the ice. The foolish bear grabbed it, and pulled himself to safety, still holding the fish.

"How can I thank you?" he asked.

"That fish would do nicely," said the smart little bear, and he strolled away to start his winter's sleep.

Pigs will be Pigs

Everyone on Old MacDonald's farm knew that it would soon be Old George's birthday. The horse had reached a great age – most of the animals couldn't even count that high!

"We must organise a special party with lots of games," Maria the sheep whispered.

"That would be fun for us," said Poppy the cow, "but George is a very old horse. I don't think he'd like it that much."

Now, a pig's mind is never far from food, so it was not surprising when Percy suggested that they have a feast! "If we all keep some of our food back each day, we'll have lots saved up by George's birthday!" he said.

Everyone agreed that a feast was a good idea. The animals found a place at the back of the barn to hide the food – well away from Old MacDonald's prying eyes!

Soon, they had a huge pile of the most tasty, delicious and scrummy things ready for the party – and they were all getting very excited as the day drew nearer.

The evening before the feast, the pile of food was massive! The animals knew that Mr and Mrs MacDonald would be going to market early the next morning – they would have the whole farmyard all to themselves.

As night fell, some of the little animals were too excited to sleep.

As the moon rose over Old MacDonald's farm, Percy found himself wide awake. He tossed and turned, and turned and tossed, trying very hard not to think about the piles of delicious food.

Now, there is nothing that makes a pig so hungry as knowing that there are good things to eat nearby. Even though he knew that the food was meant for the party, and no matter how hard he tried, Percy simply could not forget that food.

"Just a mouthful or two wouldn't matter," he said to himself. "No one would miss the odd juicy apple, or a handful of corn, would they?" Percy's mouth began to water.

Percy crept out of his sty, walking on trotter tiptoes. He reached the door of the barn. Creeeaaaaaak! He pushed it open with his nose and went inside.

"GOT YOU, PERCY PIG!" clucked Jenny the hen, jumping up from behind a bale of straw. "Percy, old thing," she grinned, "we knew you wouldn't be able to resist all this gorgeous food, so we've been on guard all week. Go straight back to bed and wait until morning." Percy blushed – he had been caught out!

The next morning, as all the animals tucked in to the fabulous feast, Percy told the others that he was sorry.

"Never you mind," they said. "Pigs will be pigs! Here, have another apple, Percy!"

Old Everest

Everest was one of the biggest horses in the world. He was also one of the strongest. When he was young, and already twice as big as other horses, he pulled the heavy cart filled with peas or potatoes, cabbages or corn, and everything grown on the farm. He took the vegetables from the farm down to the market, and he brought things from the market back to the farm. He pulled the huge machine that cut the wheat to make flour. He pulled the big plough that dug the soil, so the farmer could plant the seed that grew into wheat that made the flour... that Everest took to market. He did everything!

Everest was the best... but that was ages ago.

"So why don't you do everything now?" asked Puff the Pig.

"The farmer thinks I'm too old," said Everest, sadly. "He is trying to be kind. He thinks I need a rest."

Jacob the Lamb said, "I bet you are still stronger than anything, Everest! Nothing is as strong as you!" The huge horse lowered his head.

"Well... I am not as strong as I was, little one," smiled Everest. "Anyway, farmers don't use horses any more. They use a tractor instead!"

The big old horse had lots of time to think about when he was young and still worked on the farm. He spent most of the time now in his favourite meadow nibbling grass, and, when he grew bored with that, chasing rabbits or chickens, or biting large chunks out of the hedge.

But if Parsnip the Sheep, Waddle the Goose, or Scratchitt the Cat were in his field, he would tell them his stories. Sometimes he told the same stories again without realising, but no one minded.

But Everest still thought about the tractor. It wasn't the tractor's fault. He just wanted to work.

"Why did the farmer buy the tractor?" Puff wanted to know. Everest lowered his huge head and sighed.

"He liked the colour," said Everest.

Then one day the farmer said to Everest, "That tractor of mine! It won't start! I would ask you to help, Everest, but I suppose you are enjoying your rest." Everest shook his head from side to side.

"Even so," said the farmer, "I need to plough the field and the plough won't fit a horse, just the tractor! I don't know what to do."

Everest nudged the farmer gently over to the barn where the tractor was kept. His reins and harness were there too. The big horse picked up an old lead in his mouth and hooked it on the front of the tractor. Then, as easily as anything, he pulled out the tractor. Then he pulled the plough up behind the tractor.

"You mean you can pull both together?" said the farmer. Everest nodded his head up and down. The farmer was amazed! So the farmer hooked the plough to the tractor. Then he hooked the tractor to the horse. And Everest pulled the tractor and the tractor pulled the plough. Together they ploughed the field in the fastest time ever.

Everest was still the biggest and the strongest… and now the happiest horse in the whole world.

Hot Cross Buns!

Hot cross buns!
　Hot cross buns!
One-a-penny, two-a-penny,
　Hot cross buns!
If you have no daughters,
　Give them to your sons,
One-a-penny, two-a-penny,
　Hot cross buns!

Pease Pudding Hot

Pease pudding hot,
　Pease pudding cold,
Pease pudding in the pot,
　Nine days old.

Some like it hot,
　Some like it cold,
Some like it in the pot,
　Nine days old.

Pop Goes the Weasel

Half a pound of tuppenny rice,
　Half a pound of treacle.
That's the way the money goes,
　POP! goes the weasel.

Oats and Beans

Oats and beans and barley grow,
　Oats and beans and barley grow,
Do you or I or anyone know,
　How oats and beans and barley grow?

First the farmer sows his seeds,
　Then he stands and takes his ease,
Stamps his feet and claps his hands,
　Turns around to view the land.

Sing a Song of Sixpence

Sing a song of sixpence,
  A pocket full of rye;
Four-and-twenty blackbirds
  Baked in a pie;
When the pie was opened,
  The birds began to sing;
Wasn't that a dainty dish,
  To set before a king?

Five Little Peas

Five little peas in a pea-pod pressed,
  One grew, two grew, and so did all the rest.
They grew, and they grew, and they did not stop,
  Until one day the pod went ... POP!

Five Fat Sausages

Five fat sausages frying in a pan,
  All of a sudden one went "BANG!"
Four fat sausages, etc.
  Three fat sausages, etc.
Two fat sausages, etc.
  One fat sausage frying in a pan,
All of a sudden it went "BANG!"
  and there were NO sausages left!

Robin the Bobbin

Robin the Bobbin, the big-bellied Ben,
  He ate more meat than fourscore men;
He ate a cow, he ate a calf,
  He ate a butcher and a half;
He ate a church, he ate a steeple,
  He ate the priest and all the people!
    A cow and a calf,
      An ox and a half,
    A church and a steeple,
      And all the good people,
And yet he complained that his stomach wasn't full.

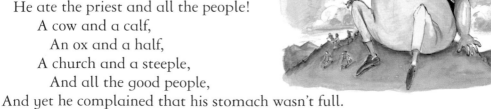

Little Dog Lost

"**B**rrr," shivered Scruffy. "It's cold tonight."

"Well, snuggle up closer to me," said his mum.

"It's not fair," Scruffy grumbled. "Why do we have to sleep outside in the cold? The cats are allowed to sleep inside, and they have nice warm baskets!"

"We're farm dogs, dear," said Mum. "We have to be tough, and work hard to earn our keep."

"I'd rather be a cat," mumbled Scruffy. "All they do is wash themselves, eat and sleep."

"We don't have such a bad life," said Mum. "Now stop feeling sorry for yourself, and get some rest. We've got a lot of work to do tomorrow."

The next day, Scruffy woke early and trotted down the lane for a walk. He ran through the grass, chasing rabbits, and sniffing at the flowers.

Now usually, when he got to the end of the lane he stopped and turned back. But today, he saw a big red van parked outside a house there. The back of the van was open, and Scruffy thought he would just climb inside and take a look.

The van was full of furniture. At the back was a big armchair with soft cushions. Scruffy clambered onto it. "I could doze all day, like a cat!" he told himself. He closed his eyes and before he knew it he had fallen fast asleep.

Scruffy awoke some time later with a sharp jolt.

"Oh, no, I fell asleep!" he groaned. "I'd better hurry back. We've got a busy day ahead!"

But then he saw that the van doors were closed! He could hear voices talking outside.

"Oh, dear, I'll be in trouble if I get found in here," thought Scruffy, and he hid behind the chair.

The back of the van opened and Scruffy peered out. Two men started unloading the furniture.

When Scruffy was sure that no one was looking, he crept out of the van, but he was no longer in the countryside where he lived! He was in a big noisy town, full of buildings and cars.

Poor Scruffy had no idea where he was!

"The van must have carried me away," thought Scruffy, feeling very frightened.

All day long, Scruffy roamed around trying to find his way home, feeling cold, tired and hungry. At last, he lay down and began to howl miserably.

"What's the matter, pup?" he heard a man's kind voice say. "You look lost. Come home with me." Scruffy gave the man's hand a grateful lick, then jumped up and followed him home.

When they arrived at the man's house Scruffy sat on the doorstep, hoping the man might bring out some food for him to eat. But the man said, "Come in, you can't stay out there."

Scruffy followed the man in, and found a little poodle waiting to meet him. Scruffy stared at her in amazement. Whatever had happened to her fur?

"You'd better take a bath before supper," said the man, looking at Scruffy's dirty white coat. The man washed him in a big tub, then brushed his tangled coat. Scruffy howled miserably. What had he done to deserve such punishment?

"Don't you like it?" asked the poodle, shyly.

"No, I don't," said Scruffy. "I think that all this washing and cleaning is for cats!"

Next the man gave them supper – small bowls of dry pellets. Scruffy looked at them and sniffed in disgust. He was used to chunks of meat and a nice big bone.

"This looks like cat food," said Scruffy, miserably.

After supper the poodle climbed into a big basket in the kitchen.

"I thought that belonged to a cat," said Scruffy. He tried sleeping in the basket but he was hot and uncomfortable. He missed counting the stars to help him fall asleep, but most of all he missed his mum.

"I want to go home," he cried, and big tears slipped down his nose.

The next day, the man put Scruffy on a lead and took him into town. He hated the way he was dragged along, without being able to stop and have a good sniff at things.

Then, as they crossed the marketplace, Scruffy heard a familiar bark, and saw his mum's head hanging through the window of the farmer's truck, parked by the side of the road! He started to howl, dragged the man over to the truck, then he leapt up at the window and barked excitedly. The farmer could hardly believe that this little dog was Scruffy – he had never seen him so clean! The man explained how he had found Scruffy, and the farmer thanked the man for taking such good care of him.

Scruffy and his mother leapt into the back of the truck. On the way back home, Scruffy told his mum all about his adventure and what had happened.

"I thought you must have run away because you didn't like being a farm dog," she said gently.

"Oh, no, Mum," said Scruffy, quickly. "I love being a farm dog. I can't wait to get home to a nice big juicy bone and our little bed beneath the stars!"

One Bad Bunny

Barney was a very bad bunny. He liked playing tricks on his friends. Barney hid Squirrel's nut store and it took him all day to find it. He put sticky honey on Badger's walking stick and Badger was chased by bees. And he put black paint on Mole's glasses, so poor Mole got even more lost than usual!

"It's time we taught that bad bunny a lesson!" said Badger crossly. So that night, while Barney was sleeping, Mole and Badger dug a big hole. Squirrel climbed up to the treetops and fetched some branches to put over the hole and they covered it with grass. They set a big juicy carrot on top, then hid behind the trees to wait.

The next morning, Barney came bouncing out of his burrow, spotted the juicy carrot and jumped straight into the trap!

"Help!" he cried, from the bottom of the hole. The others appeared.

"We tricked you!" they laughed. They only let Barney out when he promised to stop playing tricks on them. And from then on he was a very good bunny indeed.

The Naughty Broom

"Goodness me, what a lot of dirt and dust there is all over this kitchen floor," said the maid. She was a very house-proud maid, and didn't like dirt and dust on her floor one little bit. Out came the broom from its place in the cupboard in the corner, and soon the maid was busily sweeping the floor and brushing all the dirt and dust into a big dustpan.

Unfortunately, this kitchen also had elves living in it. They were too tiny to see, of course, but if you upset them they were very mischievous. As the broom worked away, it swept into one dark corner where the elves were having a party. Suddenly the king elf was swept away from their little table and into the dustpan! The next thing he knew he was being thrown, with all the other rubbish, on to the rubbish tip.

Coughing and spluttering with rage, the king elf finally climbed out from under all the rubbish and stood on top of it. He picked the dirt and dust out of his ears and nose, pulled a fish bone from out of his trousers and tried to look as king-like as he could, having just been thrown on to a rubbish tip. "Who did this?" he squeaked at the top of his voice. "I'll make someone very, very sorry indeed," he vowed.

Eventually he made his way back to the house, and into the kitchen again.

The other elves looked at the king elf and did their best not to laugh, for the king elf was still looking very dirty and untidy, with bits of rubbish stuck all over him. But the other elves knew better than to laugh at the king, because he was likely to cast a bad spell on them.

"It was the broom that did it," chorused all the other elves.

"Right," said the king elf, "then I shall cast a bad spell on the broom."

The broom was by now back in its cupboard. The king elf marched over to the cupboard and jumped in through the keyhole. The king elf pointed to the broom and said,

"*Bubble, bubble, gubble, gubble,*
Go and cause a lot of trouble!"

And with that the broom suddenly stood to attention, its bristles quivering. It was night time now and everyone in the house was asleep. The broom opened its cupboard door and sprang into the kitchen. It then unlocked the kitchen door and went outside. Straight to the rubbish tip it went, and, with a flick of its bristles, swept a huge pile of rubbish back into the kitchen. Tin cans, dirt, dust, chicken bones and goodness knows what else all got swept on to the kitchen floor.

When the maid came into the kitchen, she couldn't believe her eyes. "Who has made this awful mess?" she said. She took the broom from the cupboard and swept all the rubbish back outside again.

The next night, the same thing happened. Once it was quiet and everyone in the house was asleep, out of its cupboard came the broom, and into the house came all the rubbish again, swept there as before by the naughty broom. This time, there were fish heads, old bottles and the soot from the fireplaces.

The maid was speechless. She cleaned up again, and then she got the gardener to burn all the rubbish, so that nothing else could be brought in – although she still had no idea how it had happened.

But that night, the naughty broom decided it would make a mess in a different way. Instead of sweeping in rubbish from outside, the broom flew up to the shelves and knocked all the jars to the ground. With a crash they fell to the floor and their contents went everywhere.

"Stop this AT ONCE!" shouted a voice suddenly. "What do you think you are doing?" said the voice again.

THE NAUGHTY BROOM

The voice had come from a very stern-looking fairy who was now standing on the draining board, with her hands on her hips. What the broom did not know was that one of the bottles it had knocked down contained a good fairy, imprisoned by the elves. Now she was at last free, the spell was broken and it was her turn to cast a spell.

"Broom, broom, sweep this floor,
Make it cleaner than ever before.
Find the elves that cast your spell,
And sweep them off into the well."

The broom went to work. It swept so fast that its bristles just became a blur. It swept in every corner, and every nook and cranny. Every bit of dirt and dust, and all the broken bottles, were swept into the dustpan and then out of the house. Then it came back and swept all the elves down into the well where they couldn't do any more mischief.

In the morning, the maid came down to find a spotlessly clean kitchen. She was puzzled to find some of the jars missing, but between you and me she was also rather pleased. It just meant that there were fewer things to dust.

The New Cat

The cats on Old MacDonald's farm like nothing better than dozing. Milly just loves to laze in the sun, and Lazy, as his name suggests, hardly opens his eyes!

One day, Milly was snoozing on a bale of hay, when she heard Old MacDonald talking on the telephone through the open kitchen window. Half-asleep, she heard him say, "The new cat…" Milly was feeling very sleepy. "Yes," continued Old MacDonald, "I need it because the ones I have now are useless."

Milly yawned and stretched, still drowsy and happy. Then she suddenly sat bolt upright. What? The cats were useless? A new one was coming? Oh no!

Milly dashed to where Lazy was fast asleep and eventually woke him up! She hurriedly shouted what she had heard.

"What's the matter with us?" yawned Lazy in a hurt voice. "I don't understand."

"You don't do anything," clucked Henrietta the hen, who liked to put her beak into everybody's business. "You just sleep all day."

Milly and Lazy looked at each other. They knew there was only one thing to do. Ten seconds later, they were tearing around the farmyard, trying to look as busy as possible!

By the end of a week of dashing around all day and miaowing all night, the cats had created quite a stir in the farmyard.

"Look here," said Bruce the sheepdog. "What has got into you both?"

Milly and Lazy explained. Bruce tried not to smile. "Well, you're doing the right thing," he barked. "Impress Old MacDonald like this and you'll be fine. But I would stop the caterwauling at night."

Bruce strolled off chuckling to himself. As Old MacDonald's right-hand dog, he knew that the farmer was waiting for a new CATalogue to order his winter wellies from. But he didn't think he needed to tell Milly and Lazy that – not quite yet anyway!

Dance, Thumbkin, Dance

Dance, dance, thumbkin, dance.
  Dance ye merrymen everyone.
Thumbkin he can dance alone,
  He can dance alone.

Dance, dance, foreman, dance.
  Dance ye merrymen everyone.
Foreman he can dance alone,
  He can dance alone.

Dance, dance, longman, dance.
  Dance ye merrymen everyone.
Longman he can dance alone,
  He can dance alone.

A Face Game

Here sits the Lord Mayor; (Forehead)
  Here sit his two men;   (Eyes)
Here sits the cock;   (Right cheek)
  Here sits the hen;   (Left cheek)
Here sit the little chickens; (Tip of nose)
  Here they run in,   (Mouth)
Chinchopper, chinchopper,
  Chinchopper, chin! (Chuck the chin)

Clap Hands

Clap hands for Daddy coming
  Down the wagon way,
With a pocketful of money
  And a cartload of hay.

Wash, Hands, Wash

Wash, hands, wash,
  Daddy's gone to plough;
If you want your hands wash'd,
  Have them wash'd now.

Here's the Lady's Knives and Forks

Here's the lady's knives and forks.
 Here's the lady's table.
Here's the lady's looking glass.
 And here's the baby's cradle.
Rock! Rock! Rock! Rock!

My Hands

My hands upon my head I place,
 On my shoulders, on my face;
On my hips I place them so,
 Then bend down to touch my toe.

Now I raise them up so high,
 Make my fingers fairly fly,
Now I clap them, one, two, three.
 Then I fold them silently.

Ten Little Fingers

I have ten little fingers,
 And they all belong to me.
I can make them do things,
 Would you like to see?

I can shut them up tight,
 Or open them all wide.
Put them all together,
 Or make them all hide.

I can make them jump high;
 I can make them jump low.
I can fold them quietly,
 And hold them all just so.

Row, Row, Row Your Boat

Row, row, row your boat,
 Gently down the stream,
Merrily, merrily, merrily, merrily,
 Life is but a dream.

The Dotty Professor

Professor Von Bean was very excited. He had finished building his machine and it was ready to use. It was the most complicated contraption he had ever built and he was very proud of it.

The professor called his assistant to come to watch him start the machine. The wheels were green and brown, and there were levers on either side. The side panels were striped red and white, and there was a big chimney on the top for the smoke to escape. There was a cupboard on the side which, the professor explained, was to hang a wet coat. There was a shelf on the back for a box of plants.

While Professor Von Bean was getting more and more excited, his assistant looked very worried and puzzled.

"But what does it *do?*" he asked, timidly.

The professor scratched his head and thought.

"Oh dear, oh dear!" he sighed. "What a fool I have been! Why didn't I think of that? It does absolutely nothing useful at all!"

My Funny Family

I think that there is definitely something very strange about my family, in fact they are all very funny!

My auntie May has got a brain like a sieve, she forgets where things live. She puts a chop in the teapot and carrots in the mugs!

My uncle Fred has ears like cauliflowers, he can hear an ant whistling from a mile away, butterflies beating their wings and woodlice snoring!

My cousin Bob has eyes like a hawk, he can see from London to New York and unknown planets orbiting in space!

My brother Tom has spiders and bugs up his sleeve, which he loves to wave under my nose so that I scream.

My dog Jasper will eat anything, but especially loves fish and chips, cakes and buttered toast.

Luckily I am not so strange, I just like to dance all day!

Bouncy Bunny

Mummy Rabbit had four beautiful babies. Three of them were tiny, soft balls of fluff – they were cuddly, quiet and very, very cute. They never made a noise and always did exactly what their mummy told them.

And then there was Benny!

Benny wasn't like his brother and sisters at all. He was large and loud and he had the biggest bunny feet in the whole world. And he loved to bounce! From dawn to dusk, Benny bounced everywhere – THUMP! THUMP! THUMP! Benny never did what Mummy Rabbit told him, but she loved him just the same.

Early one morning, Mummy Rabbit was woken by a very loud noise that made the whole burrow wibble and wobble. Soon, everyone was wide awake. What was that noise?

It was Benny, of course, bouncing and boinging around the burrow on his big, flat feet! "I'm *sure* he doesn't mean to be so noisy," said Mummy Rabbit, with a big yawn.

Benny bounced outside. Mummy Rabbit followed him, twitching her nose and checking for danger – *where had he disappeared to?*

Suddenly, there was a loud THUMP! THUMP! THUMP!

"I'm hungry," said Benny, bouncing past her. "I want my breakfast now, Mummy!" By the time all the bunnies had come out of the burrow and into the sunshine, Benny had bounced round the meadow three times!

"Benny, stop jumping around!" said Mummy Rabbit. "Stay with the others. It's dangerous out here."

"Now then, children," whispered Mummy Rabbit. "We're going over to the carrot field for breakfast. You must all stay very close to me and don't wander from the path."

But, of course, Benny didn't listen. With one huge bounce he disappeared through a hole in the hedge and was gone!

"Oh, dear! Oh, dear! Oh, dear!" said his mother. "What is he up to now?"

"Benny Bunny!" said Mummy Rabbit. "Where did you get that lettuce?"

"In that field!" replied Benny.

"You might have been caught," said Mummy.

"I'm much too fast!" said Benny.

"Hurry, children," said Mummy Rabbit. "We must get to the carrot field before the farmer starts work."

But, of course, Benny wasn't listening. He was nibbling a dandelion. "Hmm, tasty!" he mumbled to himself.

"Benny Bunny!" called Mummy Rabbit, crossly. "Stop that munching and follow me!" Mummy Rabbit hopped under the gate and into the field. She collected lots of crunchy carrots. "Remember," she warned her bunnies. "Eat as much as you can, but stay close to me and watch out for the farmer."

The carrots were wonderful – fat and juicy and crisp. Soon, Benny's brother and sisters were all chewing happily. Benny bounced around on his big, flat feet, nibbling and munching as he went. Boing! Boing! Boing!

Mummy Rabbit and her bunnies munched their way across the field, nibbling a leaf here, crunching a carrot there. No one noticed that little Tufty, Benny's baby brother, wasn't following them.

Suddenly, Mummy Rabbit heard the roar of the tractor. "Quick!" she cried. "The farmer's coming!" Everyone hopped into the hedge – except Tufty!

Mummy Rabbit saw the tractor heading straight for Tufty. Its big wheels were squashing everything in its path. Her little baby crouched by the fence, his paws over his eyes, too terrified to move.

What could Mummy Rabbit do? Suddenly, Benny Bunny bounced past! In one huge bound, Benny was by Tufty's side. He bounced his brother out of the way, just before the tractor ran over him!

"I told you I was fast," giggled Benny.

"Benny Bunny!" said Mummy Rabbit, hopping over to Tufty and Benny. "You're so… "

"I know! I know!" said Benny. "I'm so *bouncy*!"

"Oh, yes!" said Mummy Rabbit. "I'm so glad that you *are* such a bouncy bunny!" and she gave him a great big kiss.

One Stormy Night

It was Patch's first night outside in his smart new kennel. He snuggled down on his warm blanket and watched as the skies grew dark. Before long he fell fast asleep. As he slept, big spots of rain began to fall. A splash of water dripped from the kennel roof on to his nose.

Just then, there was a great crash and a bright flash of light lit up the sky. Patch woke with a start and was on his feet at once, growling and snarling. "It's just a silly old storm," he told himself. "Nothing to scare a fearless farm dog like me!" But as the lightning flashed again, he saw a great shadow looming against the barn. Patch gulped. Whatever could it be? Patch began to bark furiously, trying to act braver than he felt. Next time the lightning flashed, there was no sign of the shadow. "I soon scared that monster away!" he thought.

But as Patch settled back down in his cosy kennel, the sky outside lit up once more, and there in the doorway towered the monster!

"Just checking you're okay in the storm," said Mummy, giving Patch a lick on the ear.

"A fearless farm dog like me?" said Patch. "Of course I am!" But as the storm raged on, he snuggled up close to her all the same!

Good Teamwork

It had been raining heavily for so long on Old MacDonald's farm that even the ducks wished the sun would come out.

"I shall have to take the tractor down to the bottom meadow and see if the stream is overflowing. I can't have my sheep getting wet feet!" said the farmer one morning at breakfast.

Old MacDonald set off on the tractor, but he didn't get very far. The gateway to the farmyard had become very muddy. Brrrrm! Vrrrrm! Brrrrm! The tractor did its very best, but it was soon stuck fast in the mud!

The rain trickled off Old MacDonald's nose as he climbed down from his tractor. He shook his head when he saw the mud. "Only my old friend George can help me now," he said.

Old George the horse didn't want to go out in the rain, but he stood patiently as the farmer harnessed him to the tractor.

"Now pull, George, PULL!" he cried. Old George pulled with all his might – the tractor wouldn't budge.

"I need two horses," said Old MacDonald, and he went to fetch Tilly.

Tilly and Old George pulled as hard as they could – the tractor wouldn't move. The ducks stood in a long line, watching with interest.

"If only I had another horse," said Old MacDonald. Then, before you could say "You must be joking!" the farmer had brought out his four cows to help! He tied the cows to the tractor in front of the horses and then Old George, Tilly, Annabel, Poppy, Heather and Emily pulled and pulled and pulled – the tractor still refused to move.

Old MacDonald was getting desperate. One by one, he called on Percy the pig, Maria the sheep, Bruce the sheepdog and his two cats, Milly and Lazy – and even Mrs MacDonald!

The rain continued to pour down. The MacDonalds and their animals tugged and pulled. But the tractor stayed exactly where it was!

231

The cows looked very dejected. They were sad that they hadn't been able to help.

Old MacDonald decided to have one more try. He tied everyone on to the tractor again.

Then along came Jenny the hen. "I'll help!" she clucked, and she took a very firm hold of Milly the cat's tail in her beak.

Milly howled. Lazy yowled. Bruce yelped. Maria bleated. Percy oinked. The cows mooed and the horses neighed.

Then Old MacDonald and his wife shouted above the noise of all the animals. "One, two, three, *heave*!"

And the tractor went *Squelch! Slurp! Splodge!* and rolled slowly out of the mud at last. Everyone cheered in delight and relief – and tried not to fall over in the mud!

Just at that moment, the rain stopped and a beautiful rainbow filled the sky.

"You can't beat good teamwork," beamed Old MacDonald.

"Or hens!" clucked Jenny, proudly.

Monty the Mongrel

Monty was a very curious puppy. He liked nothing better than exploring the garden.

"Don't go far," Mummy would say. But Monty wasn't worried about getting lost. He was a very good explorer.

One day, a big lorry pulled up outside the house where Monty and his family lived. Men began carrying things out of the house. One of them said something about moving, but Monty was just a puppy and didn't know what that meant.

One of the men left the gate open so, when no one was looking, Monty crept out and he had a wonderful time sniffing around other people's gardens. He found lots of yummy things to eat. And some really lovely things to roll in.

After a while, Monty began to feel tired. He was such a good explorer that he sniffed his way home with no trouble.

But when he got there, he couldn't believe his eyes. Everyone, including Mummy and all his brothers and sisters, had gone.

Monty was very surprised but he wasn't too worried. After all, he was a very good explorer. He began sniffing at once.

He soon found himself in the park where he met a group of dogs.

"Who are you?" asked one, and, "What are you?" asked another.

"Well, he's not a Poodle," sniffed the first dog, who Monty couldn't help thinking looked like a ball of cotton wool. "He's far too rough."

"He's definitely not a Dachshund," said another dog.

"He's certainly not an Old English Sheepdog," barked a third dog. "He's just not hairy enough."

"Hmm!" grunted a fourth dog, who had the flattest nose Monty had ever seen. He walked around Monty and stared at him from all sides. Then he stopped and shuddered. "Do you know what I think? I think he's a MONGREL."

"Well, if that's the case," sniffed the cotton wool dog, "he'd better hang out with Tinker."

"Take no notice of them," said Tinker. "They're just trying to help."

Monty gave Tinker a lick, and before long he was telling Tinker about his family.

"Let's walk around the park," said Tinker. "If we follow our noses, we might find your family."

In the park, Monty sniffed the air. He could smell a very familiar smell. Then, he heard a very familiar bark. Suddenly, a huge brown dog bounded out of one of the houses on the other side of the park.

"Run for your lives," yelped the cotton wool dog.

"Help! It's a giant," barked the flat-nosed dog.

"Mummy!" shouted Monty.

"Monty!" barked Mummy. "Thank goodness you're safe."

"So you're a Great Dane puppy," laughed Tinker. "Not a mongrel, after all."

Loves to Sing!

Old MacDonald loves to sing,
  Whilst doing all his chores.
His wife just thanks her lucky stars,
  He does it when outdoors!

It's rather like a lost lamb's bleat,
  A hungry horse's neigh.
The kind of snort a piglet makes,
  When rolling in the hay!

So Old MacDonald's wife just cooks,
  Her husband gets no thinner,
Because MacDonald cannot sing,
  With his mouth full of dinner!

Did You Know?

Did you know ducks like to dance?
  Their pirouettes are grand.
And what is more,
  They can perform
On water or on land.

Did you know ducks like to dance?
  They shimmy and they shake.
And what is more,
  They can perform
A very fine Swan Lake!

Busy Farmer

When a very busy farmer,
  Goes upstairs to bed at night,
He simply can't stop wondering,
  If everything's all right.

Are the cows asleep and dreaming?
  Are they trotting down the lane?
Is the cockerel in the kitchen,
  Pecking at the pies again?

So a very busy farmer,
  Always rises at first light.
He simply cannot wait to check
  That everything's all right.

Where are You?

Doris Duck, Doris Duck,
  Where are you?
Here I am! Here I am!
  Dabbling in the dew.
Dora Duck, Dora Duck,
  Where are you?
Here I am, diving down,
  Which I love to do!
Ducklings all, ducklings all,
  Where are you?
Here we are, swimming round,
  Coming to splash YOU!

Watch Out!

When Percy the pig feels peckish,
　　There's very little doubt,
That he will gobble anything,
　　Animals, watch out!
He nibbles straw
　　At the stable door.
He chomps on weed
　　Where the ducklings feed.
He munches hay
　　When the cows are away.
He snacks on corn
　　If a sack is torn.
When Percy the pig feels peckish,
　　There's very little doubt,
That even Old MacDonald
　　Shouldn't leave his lunch about!

Kittens are Cuddly

Kittens are cuddly,
　　Kittens are sweet,
They dash round the farmyard,
　　On soft, furry feet.

And before very long,
　　They are kittens no more,
But cats who do nothing,
　　But stretch out and snore!

Back to the Farm

Old MacDonald went to town,
　　Three pigs under his arm.
One didn't want to go there,
　　So he ran back to the farm.

Old MacDonald went to town,
　　Two pigs under his arm.
One kicked the farmer on his knee,
　　And ran back to the farm.

Old MacDonald went to town,
　　One pig under his arm.
He bit the farmer on the nose,
　　Then ran back to the farm.

The piglets didn't want to go,
　　They said, "We like it here!"
MacDonald said, "Oh, all right then!"
　　And the pigs began to cheer!

Without a Growl

When Old MacDonald's work is done,
And twilight falls with the setting sun,
　　He sits down in his chair.
For he knows that he has a friend,
From day's beginning to day's end,
　　Bruce the sheepdog
　　is there.

Bumble Bee Helps Out

Bumble Bee was the busiest bee in the hive. Her job was collecting flower pollen, which the other bees used to make honey. Bumble Bee had lots of friends, but she was usually far too busy to stop and chat. "Maybe tomorrow," she would cry, as she flew around from one flower to the next.

One day, Bumble Bee collected too much pollen. "I can't carry it all," she thought, "I'll ask Sammy Spider for help!"

But Sammy Spider was busy mending his web. "I'm glad you flew past!" he said. "Would you help me and hold these threads?"

So Bumble Bee helped Sammy, and they worked at the web together.

Next Bumble Bee went to find her friend Anita Ant, who was struggling with her brothers to carry a really heavy pea-pod.

"We're very glad to see you!" they cried. "Can you help us carry this pea-pod home?"

Poor Bumble Bee thought, "I need some help to carry the pollen, but perhaps this won't take very long."

So she helped the ants carry their pea-pod home.

"Now who can I find to help me?" thought Bumble Bee. Just then, she heard Lizzie Ladybird sobbing.

"I've lost my baby sister," said Lizzie. "I can't find her anywhere – will you help me look?" Bumble Bee helped Lizzie Ladybird search the woods until they found Lizzie's baby sister, lying fast asleep on a bright red leaf.

"No wonder I couldn't find you!" cried Lizzie.

At the end of the day, Bumble Bee stood looking at her pile of pollen, wondering what to do. Suddenly all of her friends arrived at once, led by Belinda Butterfly with her beautiful wings. Everyone helped her carry the pollen back to the hive.

"Oh thank you!" cried Bumble Bee.

"You helped us and now it's our turn to help you," they all replied. "That's what friends are for!"

The Yellow Digger

Crash! Bang! Clatter! There was a terrific noise in the yard at Faraway Farm. Rosie sat up in bed clutching Billy Rabbit. "What's happening?" she called. When she peeped out of the window, she saw an amazing sight. Down below, Joe the farm worker was driving the yellow digger round, scraping great holes in the yard. As Rosie watched, the digger took a mouthful of stones in its scoop. Then it spun round and clattered over to a huge dirt pile. The stones poured out making a roar like thunder. Rosie rushed downstairs, nearly tripping over Conker the dog in the hall.

"Joe's knocking down the house," she cried.

"Don't worry, Rosie," said Dad. "We're laying some new concrete in the yard. The old yard is cracked and muddy, so Joe is scraping it off. Get dressed and put your boots on. I've got a job for you and Danny."

Outside, the digger chugged backwards and forwards. "I wish I could drive it," sighed Danny.

"All in good time," said Dad. "Right now, I want you to run down to the gate and look out for the concrete truck. When it arrives, open the gate so we can get it right into the yard."

The children raced off. "I can see it!" shrieked Rosie, standing on the gate. Together, the children swung open the gate to let in a huge blue truck. The driver waved to them as he passed. The truck stopped in the yard but the concrete container went on turning with a loud scrunching sound.

"Why doesn't it stay still?" asked Rosie.

"Because all the concrete will go hard if it stops," said Dad.

The engine chugged and the concrete container churned slowly round and round. "What's going to happen now?" asked Rosie in excitement, as the driver pulled a lever and out poured the concrete. Dad and Joe spread the thick gooey mixture all over the yard.

Dad wiped his sweaty face with a handkerchief. "Phew! I'm boiling hot now. Just make sure you don't step in the concrete while it's still wet."

While Dad and Joe went inside for a cold drink, Rosie and Danny gazed at the shiny, smooth yard. "When will it dry?" asked Rosie, poking the concrete with a little stick.

"Not till tomorrow," said Danny, drawing a round smiley face.

"I'd like to go paddling in it," said Rosie. "Wouldn't you?"

Joe came out of the house and started the digger. The sudden roar made Stan the cat leap up in fright. "Oh, no!" cried Danny. "Catch him quick." Rosie grabbed but Stan was too fast. He dashed across the yard, leaving a long trail of paw prints in the wet concrete. Conker barked madly and raced after him. The children watched in horror as Conker hurtled into the wet concrete. Stan leaped neatly on to the water butt. Conker slithered to a halt as his paws sank into the thick grey mixture. Gingerly he hopped a few more steps, then stood still with a puzzled look on his face.

"Uh oh!" said Danny, glumly. "Somebody's going to be in trouble."

When Dad came out of the house and saw Conker stranded in the concrete, his face went very red and cross-looking. "Who let those animals into the yard?" he asked sternly. "Look at my lovely concrete."

Conker whimpered and tried to wag his tail. "He's very sorry," said Rosie, tugging at Dad's sleeve. "Will he have to stay there till it's dry?"

"Don't be silly," snorted Danny. "We'll never get him out then."

"I've got an idea," shouted Joe. Joe revved up the digger's engine and rumbled over to the edge of the yard. Slowly he stretched out the digger's arm, edging the scoop as near to Conker as he could. Everybody cheered. "Come on, Conker. Jump in." But Conker wouldn't budge.

"I know what to do," cried Rosie. She dashed indoors and returned with some of Conker's favourite biscuits. She put some into the digger's scoop. Then Joe stretched out the arm across the concrete again. Conker's eyes brightened. He sniffed the biscuits and then, very carefully, climbed into the scoop. Everyone held their breath.

"Up we go," said Joe, raising the digger's arm slowly. Conker started barking like mad.

"Stay still," called Rosie. For once, Conker did as he was told. When the scoop was lowered, he sprang out and shook himself, spraying everyone with wet concrete. They all laughed, even Dad.

"Ugh!" said Danny, as Conker leaped up to lick his face. "You're filthy."

"Make sure you wash those paws before you come indoors," said Dad.

Rosie slipped her hand into Dad's and whispered in his ear. "I like the yard better with all the footprints in it. Can I put my footprint in it too?" Dad smiled.

"Well, perhaps we could all put our footprint in it before it dries." Rosie clapped her hands and ran off to fetch Mum and Billy Rabbit.

Everybody put a footprint in the wet concrete. Billy Rabbit's was the smallest and Joe's enormous boot was the biggest. Then Dad got a stick and they each wrote their initials next to the footprint. "I'll write Conker's because he can't spell," said Danny.

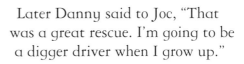

Later Danny said to Joe, "That was a great rescue. I'm going to be a digger driver when I grow up."

"I'm going to be a vet," said Rosie, hugging Conker.

"Come on then," laughed Mum. "I think it's time we gave that naughty dog a bath."

A Perfect Puppy

Molly had wanted a puppy for a long time, so when Mummy and Daddy said yes, she couldn't wait to get to the pet shop.

At the pet shop, Polly inspected the puppies one by one. After all, her puppy had to be perfect.

"That one's too big," said Polly, pointing to a Great Dane. "And that one's too small." She pointed to a tiny Chihuahua.

"This one's nice," said the shopkeeper, patting a Poodle.

"Too curly," Polly declared.

Another puppy was too noisy. And one was too quiet. Before long, there weren't many puppies left. Polly was about to give up, when something soft rubbed against her leg.

"Ah, perfect," she cried, picking up a small bundle of black and white fur.

"Err, what kind of puppy is it?" asked Daddy.

"It's my puppy," sighed Polly.

"It's a mongrel," said the shopkeeper. "I think it's part Spaniel and part Collie. We're not really sure."

"I don't care what he is," smiled Polly. "He's just perfect. I'm going to call him Danny."

A Perfect Puppy

Danny whined as he left the pet shop. And he whined all the way home. He stopped whining when he saw the cat and barked instead.

"He'll be okay once he gets used to us," said Mummy. Polly hoped she was right.

In the afternoon, they took Danny for a walk. Polly took some bread to feed the ducks, but as soon as Danny saw the ducks he started to bark. Then he began to chase them and didn't stop until they had all flown away.

Daddy bought Polly an ice cream to cheer her up.

"He's just a puppy. He's got a lot to learn," explained Daddy as Danny jumped up and stole her ice cream. Polly was beginning to wonder if she'd chosen the right puppy.

When they got home, Polly decided to introduce Danny to all her dolls and cuddly toys, but Danny pounced on her favourite teddy.

"He's got Mr Fluffy," cried Polly, as Danny raced from the room into the garden. When he came back, Mr Fluffy was gone.

Polly was furious. She waved an angry finger at Danny. "You're not a perfect puppy," she said. "I don't think you'll ever learn."

Poor Danny, he hung his head and slunk away under the table and wouldn't come out all evening.

The next morning, Polly was woken up by something wet pressed against her cheek. It was Danny, and in his mouth was Mr Fluffy! Danny dropped Mr Fluffy on the floor for Polly to pick up.

"Good boy, Danny," laughed Polly, tickling his ears. "You are a perfect puppy, after all!"

Birthday Bear

Rosie woke up, jumped out of bed and ran into Danny's room. "Guess what day it is!"

"It's Saturday," muttered Danny, grumpily. "And it's raining too."

"I know it's Saturday, silly," exclaimed an excited Rosie. "But it's my birthday!" Rosie spotted Jack the postman coming up the path. She ran downstairs to meet him.

"There's nothing for you," he teased. But Jack's bag was bulging!

"You can open your cards when Daddy comes in," laughed Mum. "But the birthday girl needs her breakfast first."

After breakfast, they all watched while Rosie opened a great pile of cards and presents. "I've got a card from Conker," said Rosie and gave

him a big kiss. "It's got his paw mark on!"

They spent the morning getting the house ready for Rosie's birthday party.

They blew up balloons and hung up streamers until everything looked perfect.

"That looks lovely," announced Mum, finally. "I can see Joe down by the pond. Why don't you go and feed the ducks while I finish everything else."

Danny and Rosie ran through the orchard and waved to Joe the farm worker. It had stopped raining but it was still very wet and muddy. "Happy birthday, Rosie," called Joe. When they reached the pond, Rosie noticed something floating at the edge of the water all tangled up in the weeds.

"What's that muddy blob over there?" she asked.

"I'll go in and see," said Danny, splashing into the pond and wading out towards the curious object. Dan took three steps, then stopped.

"Go on," called Rosie. "What's the matter?" Danny began to giggle.

"I can't move," he said. "My boots are stuck in the mud!" Rosie started to laugh too. Danny wriggled, pulled, twisted and turned, trying to free his boots from the mud. Suddenly, Danny's foot slipped out of his boot and he sat in the water with a huge splash. Joe came across to see what all the laughter was about and held out his hand to Danny.

"What's that muddy mess you're holding?" he chuckled.

"I don't know," replied a very wet and muddy Danny, pulling weeds out of his hair. "Here you can have it, Rosie."

"It's a bear!" cried Rosie, cuddling the soggy bundle. "A poor muddy old bear."

"I wonder how he got there?" asked Danny. Dripping wet and covered with mud, Danny and Rosie walked back to the house.

"What have you been up to?" laughed Mum. "And who is this little fellow?" Mum took the bear from Rosie. "Oh dear! I think all three of you need a bath before the party starts." In no time at all, Rosie, Danny and the little bear were ready for the party.

"Wow! Look at the cake, Rosie," said Danny. "It looks brilliant!"

Rosie tied a big yellow bow around the bear's neck and sat him on the window sill to watch the party.

At bedtime, Rosie sighed, "That was the best birthday party ever. I love being five. Do you know what my best present was, Mummy?" she added.

"What was that?" asked Mum.

"It was that poor old muddy bear. I wish I could keep him."

"Well, we'll have to wait and see," said Mum. "He might belong to someone."

The next day, Rosie made a "Lost Bear" poster and Jack put it in the post office window. Nobody came to collect the bear, so Rosie adopted him. Rosie made up lots of stories about how the bear got into the pond. But they never did find out.

"It doesn't matter where you came from," she told him. "You can live with us now. Billy Rabbit can be your best friend."

"What will you call him?" asked Danny.

"Birthday Bear, of course!"

Chalk and Cheese

Chalk and Cheese were as different as two kittens can be. Chalk was a fluffy white kitten, who liked dishes of cream and lazing in the sun. Cheese was a rough, tough black kitten, who liked chewing on fish tails and climbing trees. Their mother puzzled over her odd little pair of kittens, but she loved them both the same.

One day, Cheese climbed high up on the barn and got stuck. "Help!" he cried to his sister.

"I don't like climbing!" she said, opening one eye.

"If only you were more like me!" said Cheese, "you'd be able to help!"

"If only you were more like me," said Chalk, "you wouldn't have got stuck in the first place!" And with that she went back to sleep. Just then, the farm dog came by. Chalk sprang up as he gave a loud bark and began to chase her.

"Help!" she cried to Cheese, up on the barn.

"I'm stuck, remember?" he cried. "You shouldn't lie where dogs can chase you."

Then Mummy appeared. She swiped the dog away with her claws, then climbed up and rescued Cheese.

"If only you were more like me," she said, "you'd keep out of danger and look after each other." And from then on, that's just what they did.

Alone

From childhood's hour I have not been
   As others were, — I have not seen
As others saw, — I could not bring
   My passions from a common spring.
From the same source I have not taken
   My sorrow; I could not awaken
My heart to joy at the same tone;
   And all I loved, I loved alone.
Then – in my childhood – in the dawn
   Of a most stormy life was drawn
From every depth of good and ill
   The mystery which binds me still:
From the torrent, or the fountain,
   From the red cliff of the mountain,
From the sun that round me rolled
   In its autumn tint of gold, –
From the lightning in the sky
   As it passed me flying by, –
     From the thunder and the storm,
      And the cloud that took the form
(When the rest of Heaven was blue)
   Of a demon in my view.

EDGAR ALLAN POE

All the Bells Were Ringing

All the bells were ringing
   And all the birds were singing,
When Molly sat down crying
   For her broken doll.

O you silly Moll!
   Sobbing and sighing
   For a broken doll,
When all the bells are ringing
   And all the birds are singing.

CHRISTINA ROSSETTI

There Was an Old Man With a Beard

There was an old Man with a beard,
   Who said, "It is just as I feared! –
Two Owls and a Hen, four Larks and a Wren
   Have all built their nests in my beard!"

EDWARD LEAR

Hurt No Living Thing

Hurt no living thing,
  Ladybird nor butterfly,
Nor moth with dusty wing,
  Nor cricket chirping cheerily,
Nor grasshopper, so light of leap,
  Nor dancing gnat,
  Nor beetle fat,
Nor harmless worms that creep.

CHRISTINA ROSSETTI

Bread and Milk for Breakfast

Bread and milk for breakfast,
  And woollen frocks to wear,
And a crumb for robin redbreast
  On the cold days of the year.

CHRISTINA ROSSETTI

Going Downhill on a Bicycle

With lifted feet, hands still,
  I am poised, and down the hill
Dart, with heedful mind;
  The air goes by in a wind.

Swifter and yet more swift,
  Till the heart with a mighty lift
Makes the lungs laugh,
    the throat cry:–
  "O bird, see; see, bird, I fly.

"Is this, is this your joy?
  O bird, then I, though a boy,
For a golden moment share
  Your feathery life in air!"

Say, heart, is there aught like this
  In a world that is full of bliss?
'Tis more than skating, bound
  Steel-shod to the level ground.

Speed slackens now, I float
  Awhile in my airy boat;
Till, when the wheels scarce crawl,
  My feet to the treadles fall.

Alas, that the longest hill
  Must end in a vale; but still,
Who climbs with toil, wheresoe'er,
  Shall find wings waiting there.

HENRY CHARLES BEECHING

253

Barney the Boastful Bear

Barney was a very boastful bear. "Look at my lovely soft fur!" he would say to the other toys. "See how it shines!"

Barney loved to talk about himself. "I'm the smartest toy in the playroom!" he would say. "It's a well-known fact."

He didn't know that the other toys all laughed about him behind his back.

"That bear thinks he's so smart," growled Scotty Dog. "But he isn't smart enough to know when everyone's fed up with him!"

"He'll learn his lesson one of these days," said Molly Monkey, and sure enough, that is just what happened...

One hot summer's day, the toys lazed in the warm playroom. "Wouldn't it be lovely if we could all go for a walk outside," said Rag Doll.

"We could have a lovely picnic in the woods!" said Old Bear.

"Even better, we could all go for a drive in the toy car first!" said Rabbit.

"But none of us is big or clever enough to drive the toy car," said Rag Doll, sadly.

"I am!" came a voice from the corner. It was Barney. He had been listening to them talking.

"I can drive the toy car. And I know the best place for a picnic in the woods," he said.

"We've never seen you drive the car," said Rabbit, suspiciously.

"That's because I drive it at night, when you're asleep," said Barney. "I'm a very good driver, in fact."

"Ooh, let's go then!" cried Rag Doll. And in no time they had packed up a picnic and were sitting ready in the car.

"Er, I don't feel like driving today, actually," mumbled Barney. "It's too hot." But the others were not interested in hearing excuses, so rather reluctantly Barney climbed into the driver's seat and started the engine. You see, the truth was, Barney had never really driven the car before, and he was scared. But he wanted to show off, so he pretended to know what he was doing.

Off they set down the garden path. "Toot, toot!" Barney beeped the horn as he turned the little car out into the country lane, and soon they were driving along, singing merrily.

All was going well, until Rag Doll suddenly said, "Hey, Barney, didn't we just miss the turning for the woods?"

"I know where I'm going," said Barney, crossly. "Leave it to me." And he made the little car go faster.

"Slow down a bit, Barney!" called Old Bear, from the back seat. "My fur is getting all ruffled." He was starting to feel anxious.

"I don't need a back-seat driver, thank you," said Barney, with a growl, and made the car go even faster. By now the others were starting to feel

scared, but Barney was having a great time.

"Aren't I a wonderful driver!" he chuckled. "Look – no hands!" And he took his paws off the steering wheel. Just then they reached

a sharp corner. The little car went spinning off the side of the road and crashed into a tree, tipping all the toys out into the ditch!

They were a bit dazed, but luckily no one was hurt. They were not pleased with Barney though.

"You're a silly bear!" said Rabbit, crossly. "We could all have been badly hurt!"

"We'll have to walk home now," said Rag Doll, rubbing her head. "Where are we?"

Everyone looked at Barney.

"Don't ask me!" he said, quietly.

"But you told us that you knew the way!" said Old Bear, indignantly.

"I was only pretending," said Barney,

his voice trembling. "I don't really know how to drive, and I don't know where we are!" And he started to cry.

The other toys were furious with Barney.

"You naughty boastful bear!" they scolded. "Now see what trouble your boasting has got us into!"

The lost toys walked through the dark woods all night long, clinging together in fright as shadows loomed around them.

They had never been out at night before. Then just before dawn, they spotted the little house where they lived, and crept back into the playroom.

What a relief it was to be home again!

Luckily their owner had not noticed they were missing, so she never knew what an adventure her toys had been having while she was fast asleep. She often wondered what had happened to her toy car though.

Little Chick Lost

"Stay close, Little Chick!" said Mummy, as they set out to visit Mrs Duck, who lived on the pond. Little Chick tried to keep up with Mummy, but there were so many interesting things to look at that he soon got lost in the long grass.

He was busy amongst the toadstools watching a shiny beetle climb slowly up a stem of grass, when a dark shadow fell over him. He looked up to see a huge mouth coming silently towards him! It was a fox, and he looked rather hungry!

"Help!" cried Little Chick, looking around for somewhere to hide.

Just then, Spot, the farm dog, appeared and with a great woof he chased the fox away. He was good at protecting the farm animals.

Mummy arrived flapping her wings. "I told you to stay close," she said, tucking Little Chick safely under her wing.

And from then on, that is just where Little Chick stayed!

Snowy and Blowy

Old MacDonald peered out of his window and decided to put on three extra jumpers.

"That's very sensible," said Mrs MacDonald. "You need to keep warm when it's snowy."

"What worries me," said Old MacDonald, "is that it's snowy *and* blowy. I must make sure that the sheep are safe. They really don't like it when the snow gets blown into heaps in the fields. It's time they came down from the meadow."

Old MacDonald puffed and panted as he put on his boots and set off for the meadow, taking Bruce the sheepdog with him.

But when they reached the meadow, the sheep were nowhere to be seen. They were completely hidden by the snow!

"On days like these," said Old MacDonald, "I wish I had black sheep instead of white ones."

Suddenly, Bruce started to behave in a very strange way, jumping up and down with his paws together, just like sheep do!

Old MacDonald understood, he laughed and patted Bruce's head. Then he shouted, "Today there is going to be a jumping competition to keep us all warm! I think the rabbits in the next field will win!"

Woosh! One energetic sheep jumped up, showering snow all around. Woosh! Woosh! Two more leapt into the air, shaking the snow from their coats. Suddenly, the field was full of leaping, jumping sheep!

Those sheep made quite sure that the rabbits in the next field didn't stand a chance. Actually, those rabbits were all snugly sleeping in their burrows, quite unaware that their honour as jumpers was at stake.

Back in the farmyard, the other animals saw how warm and happy the woolly jumpers were. Before long, everyone joined in, even Henry, much to the embarassment of the hens. The farmyard was full of laughing, smiling animals bouncing up and down – a very strange sight.

Of course, Old MacDonald didn't join in. He was too busy puffing and panting again, trying to get his boots off. All he wanted to do was to get in the warm of the farmhouse and settle down by the fire. He could smell his lunch and all that walking in the wind and the snow had made him very hungry!

And of course Bruce was too busy thinking about his bone to stay out in the yard with all those bouncing animals. His empty tummy was far more important!

Easter Bunnies

It was Easter and the naughty bunnies had hidden eggs for the animals to find. How they chuckled when they saw the farm cat shaking water from her fur. She had been searching by the pond and had fallen in! The bunnies giggled as they watched the hens shooing the pig away from the hen house. "They're not in here!" the hens clucked.

Eventually, when the animals had searched high and low, Daisy the cow said, "It's no use, we can't find them! We give up!"

"Here's a clue," said the bunnies. "Where do you find eggs?"

"In a nest," answered Mrs Goose.

"And what do you make a nest with?" asked the bunnies.

"Straw!" said the horse.

"They must be in the haystack!" cried all the animals at once.

They rushed to the field and there, hidden in the haystack, was a pile of lovely Easter eggs.

What a feast they had!

Old Joe Brown

Old Joe Brown, he had a wife,
  She was all of eight feet tall.
She slept with her head in the kitchen,
  And her feet stuck out in the hall.

Poor Old Robinson Crusoe!

Poor old Robinson Crusoe!
  Poor old Robinson Crusoe!
They made him a coat
  Of an old nanny goat,
I wonder how they could do so!
  With a ring a ting tang,
  And a ring a ting tang,
    Poor old Robinson Crusoe!

Old John Muddlecombe

Old John Muddlecombe lost his cap,
  He couldn't find it anywhere, the poor old chap.
He walked down the High Street, and everybody said,
  "Silly John Muddlecombe, you've got it on your head!"

Michael Finnegan

There was an old man called Michael Finnegan,
  He grew whiskers on his chinnegan.
The wind came out and blew them in again,
  Poor old Michael Finnegan. Begin again...

Rub-a-dub Dub

Rub-a-dub dub,
  Three men in a tub,
And who do you think they be?
  The butcher, the baker,
The candle-stick maker,
  Turn them out knaves all three.

Tommy Thumb

Tommy Thumb, Tommy Thumb,
  Where are you?
Here I am, here I am,
  How do you do?

Peter Pointer, Peter Pointer,
  Where are you?
Here I am, here I am,
  How do you do?

Middle Man, Middle Man,
  Where are you?
Here I am, here I am,
  How do you do?

Ruby Ring, Ruby Ring,
  Where are you?
Here I am, here I am,
  How do you do?

Baby Small, Baby Small,
  Where are you?
Here I am, here I am,
  How do you do?

Fingers all, fingers all,
  Where are you?
Here we are, here we are,
  How do you do?

Solomon Grundy

Solomon Grundy,
  Born on Monday,
Christened on Tuesday,
  Married on Wednesday,
Sick on Thursday,
  Worse on Friday,
Died on Saturday,
  Buried on Sunday,
That was the end
  Of Solomon Grundy.

Jack Sprat

Jack Sprat could eat no fat,
  His wife could eat no lean,
And so between the two of them
  They licked the platter clean.

Clumsy Fred

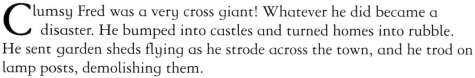

Clumsy Fred was a very cross giant! Whatever he did became a disaster. He bumped into castles and turned homes into rubble. He sent garden sheds flying as he strode across the town, and he trod on lamp posts, demolishing them.

Everyone ran whenever Clumsy Fred was approaching. They could hear him coming for miles as he crashed and banged his way across the countryside and through the town.

People became more and more concerned, what was the matter with Fred? He used not to be so clumsy, and in fact for a one-eyed giant he was a very friendly chap. There was definitely something wrong, but no one was sure how to help.

Then a monster expert came to the rescue. He went to see Fred, who was feeling very sad. "Why am I so clumsy?" he asked. "I don't like upsetting everyone, but I just can't help it!"

The expert did a lot of tests, and found the solution. "I know what is wrong!" he said. "The problem is your eye!"

So Fred put on a monocle and suddenly he could see. He wasn't clumsy any more, and Fred was as happy as can be!

Oscar the Octopus

Oscar the Octopus was a keen footballer, he loved rushing about the field. With his many feet he was a real menace to the other team. Today was a big match, and he was playing at number eleven.

Oscar began to get ready, he stretched out a tentacle and put on the first boot, then he put on the second. As Oscar put on boot three the crowds had begun to gather beside the sea to watch the match. He could hear them singing their song about Oscar, the latest goal-scoring sensation. As Oscar put on boot four he was feeling on top form. On went boot five as the crowd swayed and cheered loudly. The harder Oscar tried to hurry, the longer it seemed to take!

Boot number six went on, and Oscar stood on his head and practised some tricks, then boot seven – he was almost ready. Now it was the last one – boot eight. Oscar was getting nervous and the laces were so fiddly that it took him ages.

At last he was ready and on to the pitch he went, ready for his debut in front of the crowd. But the referee said, "Sorry Oscar! You're too late. The game is over, the whistle has blown. Nobody scored and the crowd has gone home!"

Mr Mole Gets Lost

Mr Mole poked his little black nose out from the top of one of his molehills and took a great big sniff of the air. Then he sniffed again. And then a third time, just to make sure. "Oh dear," he thought, "it smells as though it's going to rain."

Mr Mole didn't like the rain one bit. Every time he got caught in the rain his plush little velvet fur coat got all wet and drippy, and he left muddy footprints all over his underground burrow. But worse still, the rain got in through the holes in his molehills and then everything got all soggy and took days to dry out.

Well, the skies got darker and darker, and very soon little spots of rain began to fall. Then the spots became bigger. And then bigger still. Before long, all you could see before your eyes were big, straight rods of rain bouncing off the leaves on the trees, pounding the ground and turning everything muddy and wet.

Mr Mole had never seen rain like it. He sat in his burrow in the middle of the meadow wishing it would stop. But it just kept raining and raining.

Soon the rain started entering his burrow. First it went drip, drip, drip through the holes in his molehills, and then it became a little river of water in the bottom of his burrow. Then the little river became a bigger, faster-flowing river and suddenly it was carrying Mr Mole along with it. Through the tunnels of his burrow he went, this way and then that, as the water gushed and poured through his underground home.

The next thing he knew he was being washed out of his burrow completely as the rain water carried him off down the meadow. Down he went, not knowing which way up he was or where he was going. Now he was being washed through the woods at the bottom of the meadow, but still the water carried him on, bouncing and turning him until he was dizzy and gasping for breath.

Suddenly, he came to a halt. The rain water gurgled and trickled around him and then flowed onwards, as he found himself stuck firmly in the branches of a bush.

"Oh dear," Mr Mole said as he got himself free. "Goodness me, where can I be?" he thought. Mr Mole looked around him, but being a very short-sighted mole – as most moles are – he couldn't make out any of the places that were familiar to him. Worse still, he couldn't smell any smells that were familiar to him. He was completely lost, far from home, and had no idea how to get back again. Now, to make things worse, it was starting to get dark.

"Woo-oo-oo-oo-oo!" said a voice suddenly. Mr Mole nearly jumped out of his moleskin with fright.

"I wouldn't stay here if I were you. Don't you know it isn't safe in the woods at night?" said the voice. "There are snakes, foxes and weasels and all sorts of nasty creatures, that you really wouldn't like to meet."

Mr Mole looked up and found himself face to face with a huge owl.

"Oh dear!" was all Mr Mole could think of saying. He told the owl of his terrible watery journey and how he was lost and didn't know how to get back home again.

"You need to talk to Polly Pigeon," said the owl. "She is a homing pigeon and she lives near your meadow. She can show you the way home. But we'll have to find her first. Stay close to me, mind, and look out for those snakes, foxes and weasels I told you about."

Mr Mole didn't need telling twice. He stayed so close to the kindly owl that, every time the owl stopped or turned round to talk to Mr Mole, Mr Mole bumped right into him!

Through the dark, dangerous woods they went. Every now and again, there would be an unfriendly noise, such as a deep growl or a hiss, coming from the dense, tangled trees, but Mr Mole didn't want to think about that too much, so he just made sure that he never lost sight of the owl.

Finally, just when Mr Mole thought that he couldn't go a step further, they came to a halt by an old elm tree.

"Hallo-oooo," called the owl.

They were in luck. Polly Pigeon was about to continue her journey home.

"Please," said Mr Mole, "I'm afraid I'm terribly lost and don't know how to get back to my meadow. Will you take me there?"

"Of course I will," said Polly Pigeon. "We'd better let you rest here a while first, though. But we must go before it gets light."

So Mr Mole was soon trudging wearily back to his meadow, following as closely behind Polly Pigeon as he was able. Just as the first rays of sun lit the morning sky, Mr Mole smelled a very familiar smell. It was his meadow! He was almost home!

Soon, he was back in his own burrow. It was so wet and muddy that the first thing he did was dig some new tunnels in the top of the meadow so that the rain wouldn't wash down into them so easily. Then he settled down to eat one of his supplies of worms, and fell into a deep, well-earned slumber.

Not Another Bear

William loved teddy bears. When asked what he would like for his birthday, or for Christmas, William's answer was always the same, "I'd like a teddy bear, please."

"Not another bear!" his parents would say. "Look at your bed, William. There's no room for any more!" It was true. There were bears all over William's bed. Every night William had to squeeze into the tiny space that was left. But William didn't mind at all.

"We've got to do something about this," said William's dad, marching into William's bedroom with a pile of wood and a bag of tools. "We'll make some shelves, so that you can have some room." By tea time there were three shelves on William's bedroom wall. And a row of bears sat neatly on each one. When William went to bed that night there was plenty of room. But it just didn't feel right.

Next day, at the school fair, Mum gave William some pocket money. "Find something you'd like," she said. William noticed a small bear on the White Elephant stall. He bought it and when they got home he ran straight upstairs. "What did you buy, William?" Mum called up. William grinned.

"Not another bear!" sighed Mum.

"But there's plenty of room now," William answered. He winked at the new bear, and William was sure that the bear winked back.

Yes, You Can!

Ozzie sat on the river bank watching the other otters having fun. He wished he could splash in the water like them. But Ozzie didn't dare to go down into the river, because he couldn't swim! Once, he climbed to the top of the bank and looked at the water below. But he had been really scared so, since then, he always sat by the river on his own.

"What's the matter, Ozzie?" asked his mum.

"I wish I could swim so I could have fun with my friends," said Ozzie.

"But you can," laughed Mum. "Come on," she said. "Climb on my back and hold tight." So, with Ozzie holding on to his mum's back, they slipped into the water and swam round in small circles. At first, Ozzie was frightened. Then, he began to enjoy the water, lapping at his sides.

"This is fun!" he cried. "Can we do it again?" But there was no answer. Ozzie's mum wasn't there. She was on the river bank, smiling at him.

"Help!" yelled Ozzie, in panic. "I can't swim!"

"Yes, you can," called his mum. "Pretend you're running!" Suddenly, he felt himself moving forward – he was swimming! Round and round he went, splashing and diving.

On the bank, he found a tiny otter shivering. "What's the matter?" asked Ozzie.

"I can't swim," said the otter.

"Yes, you can!" smiled Ozzie. "Come on, climb on my back and I'll show you!"

Bottoms Up!

The time had come for Doris the duck to teach her ducklings to dive. "It's easy, little ducklings," she quacked. "You bob your heads under the water and put your bottoms in the air. Just remember that – heads down, bottoms up!"

The ducklings nodded excitedly and had a go. Quite a few managed it first time.

"Oooh!" squeaked one. "There are lots of interesting things down there!"

"Exactly!" cried Doris. "And that is why you must all learn to dive. Only we ducks know what goes on under the water."

All afternoon, the ducklings practised. Heads down! Bottoms up! One by one, they got the hang of it.

"Oh, Mummy, look! There are tiny fishes flashing about under here!" squealed one.

"And there's an old bucket, too!" called out another.

"I've found a squiggly thing," quacked a third, "and it tastes lovely!"

By teatime, all the ducklings could dive except for one.

"What's the matter, Dylan?" asked Doris.

"I'm afraid I might not come up again," whispered the little duckling.

"But, Dylan," quacked Doris, "to pop right up again, all you have to do is put your head up and your bottom down!"

Even so, Dylan still didn't want to try. Doris was as encouraging as she could be, but, when the sun began to set, even she was becoming a little bit impatient.

"All ducks dive, Dylan," she said. "You just have to do it. Go on! One, two, three, DIVE!"

But still Dylan hesitated. "I'm going to be one of those ducks who doesn't dive," he said. "I can't see the point. I'm not sure I want to stick my head under the water, it's cold down there. And I might not be able to put my head up again when my tail is up in the air. And I don't want to catch lots of squiggly wiggly things, even if they do taste nice, they might tickle my beak!"

Doris didn't say a word. Then she had an idea…

"Supper time!" called Doris. All the little ducklings bobbed their heads up.

"We're not hungry!" they called. "We've been eating fishes and squiggly things and delicious duckweed all day."

"I haven't," said Dylan. "I'm really hungry."

So Doris dived down and found him a nice fish.

"Here you are, Dylan," she quacked as she bobbed up. "Oops!"

As Doris spoke, the fish dropped from her beak and disappeared into the water.

"My supper!" cried Dylan. Down went his head! Up went his bottom! And he dived quickly down and caught his dinner.

"I did it!" he cried, bobbing up again.

"Well done!" laughed Doris, happily. "But please don't talk with your mouth full, dear!"

Home Sweet Home

Bella Bunny looked at the sweet green grass growing in the meadow on the far side of the stream. She was tired of eating the rough grass that grew near her burrow. "I'm going to cross the stream!" she said to her brothers and sisters, pointing to a fallen branch that lay across it.

Bella bounced safely across the branch and was soon eating the sweet, juicy grass on the other side of the stream. Her brothers and sisters thought she was very brave and wondered if they should follow. But just then, they saw a sly fox creeping up behind Bella through the grass!

"Look out!" they called.

Bella turned to see the fox just in time! She leapt back onto the branch, but she was in such a hurry that she slipped and fell into the stream. Luckily, Becky Beaver had been watching and she pulled Bella safely to the other side.

"Home sweet home!" gasped Bella, with relief. And she ran off to join her brothers and sisters, vowing never to leave home again.

Moo! Moo! Moo!

The Meadow Ladies Chorus,
Is something rather new.
You'll hear them all too clearly,
They're singing, "Moo! Moo! Moo!"

They try to trill like budgies,
And copy blackbirds, too.
The only song they really know,
Of course, is, "Moo! Moo! Moo!"

They practise in the morning,
And in the night-time, too.
It doesn't make a difference though,
They still sing, "Moo! Moo! Moo!"

You Need a Cow!

How does fresh milk reach your shake,
The frothy, creamy kind you make?
    You ask how? – You need a cow!
How does butter reach your bread,
The slithery, slippery stuff you spread?
    You ask how? – You need a cow!
How does your cheese reach your plate,
The yummy, yellow kind you grate?
    You ask how? – You need a cow!
How does ice cream reach your spoon,
The kind you cannot eat too soon?
    You ask how? – You need a cow!

Counting Sheep

Old MacDonald's counting sheep,
    But not because he cannot sleep.
You see, he's wondering if maybe,
    Each sheep has now had her baby.
"Stand still!" he cries. "Be still and steady,
    I might have counted you already!"
Poor Old MacDonald's feeling dizzy!
Then suddenly he starts to smile.
    "Goodbye! I'll see you in a while."
When all the farm is soundly sleeping,
    Old MacDonald's softly creeping.
It's really easy to count sheep,
    When you're awake and they're asleep!

Woolly Coats

In the middle of the winter,
    All the animals complain,
"Our furry coats are much too thin.
    They let the icy north wind in.
We want to go indoors again!"
But while the rest all shiver,
    Sheep are fine and look quite smu
"We will not come to any harm.
    We are the warmest on the farm.
Our woolly coats will keep us snug!"

Clip, Clop!

Pigs can prance,
    And ducks can dance,
Hens flutter in a flurry.
But George plods on and doesn't stop,
    Clip, clop! Clip, clop!
    He's *never* in a hurry.

"Of course, I know
    My horse is slow,
But I will never worry.
For George plods on and doesn't stop,
    Clip, clop! Clip, clop!
    He doesn't *need* to hurry."

Egg Hatching Dream

When Jenny is sitting,
    And sitting, and sitting,
She can't take up knitting,
    Or sew a fine seam.

If her eggs are to hatch,
    Every one of the batch,
There is nothing to match,
    An egg-hatching dream.

Her thoughts travel far and near.
    Half-asleep she'll appear,
Until she starts to hear,
    Her eggs start to crack!

A Horse, of Course!

Who can you trust when the
        tractor breaks down,
And the nearest mechanic is
        off in the town?
Who is as big and as strong as a horse?
    Oh, silly me, a horse, of course!
Who do you know who can eat
        tons of hay,
And even munch ten sacks of oats
        in a day?
Who has an appetite large as a horse?
    Oh, silly me, a horse, of course!
Who will stick by you when you
        need a friend,
And hear all your troubles right through
        to the end?
Who is as wise and as kind as a horse?
    Oh, silly me, a horse, of course!

One Hen Pecking

One hen pecking in the garden –
    Mrs MacDonald shakes her head.
Two hens pecking in the garden –
    Makes her shake her fist instead!
Three hens pecking in the garden –
    The farmer's wife comes storming out.
Four hens pecking in the garden –
    Mrs MacDonald starts to shout.

Honey Bear and the Bees

One day, as Honey Bear woke from her dreams, her furry little nose started to twitch with excitement. She could smell her most favourite thing in the world – sweet, yummy honey! The smell was coming from a hollow tree stump nearby. She padded over and dipped in a large paw. How delicious the sweet, sticky honey tasted!

Honey Bear dipped her paw in again and again, digging deep into the tree stump to reach more of the lovely, sticky honey. This was the life! In fact, she dug so deep that, when she tried to take her great paw out, she found it was stuck fast! Just then, she heard a loud buzzing noise and looked up to see a huge swarm of angry bees returning to their hive!

Poor Honey Bear hollered as the bees flew around, stinging her all over! She tugged and tugged and at last she pulled her paw free. The angry bees chased her all the way to the river where she sat cooling her burning skin. Just then an irresistible smell reached her furry nose. It was coming from a hollow tree nearby.

"Mmm, honey!" said Honey Bear. "I'll just go and take a look…"

A Scary Adventure

It was a sunny morning at Faraway Farm.
Danny and Rosie were sitting on the grass. "I'm bored," yawned
Danny. "There's nothing to do. I want to have an adventure."

"I want to have one too," exclaimed Rosie. Then
added, "But not too scary."

"It has to be a bit scary to be exciting,"
insisted Danny. He whistled to Conker. "Here
boy!" he called. "We're off to the woods."

"Can I come too?" asked Rosie.

"No," replied Danny. "Adventures are just
for big people and dogs."

On their way to the woods, Danny and Conker
stopped to say hello to Archie who was happily
munching grass in his field. "Come on, Conker," said Danny. "Let's
make a den. It will be our secret place where we can watch out for
enemies." Danny and Conker hid in the den and kept watch. "Ssssh!"
whispered Danny. "Someone's coming." They sprang out. Conker barked
and Danny shouted "Gotcha!"

"It's only me, silly," said Rosie. "I want to have an adventure too."
Danny thought for a moment.

"All right," he agreed. "If you bring some food and drink, you can come in the den." Danny and Conker settled down to wait while Rosie ran back to the farm to see what she could get from Mum.

"It's a bit quiet, Conker," whispered Danny nervously. "Quite scary, really." Suddenly, Conker sat up. The hair on Danny's neck stood on

end. Rustle! Rustle! A twig snapped and then the roof of the den began to shake. "What's that noise?" whispered Danny. Conker began to bark. "Let's get out of here, Conker!" yelled Danny. They raced out of the den as fast as they could and bumped straight into Rosie.

"What's the matter? Where are you going?" asked Rosie, picking herself up.

"There's a monster attacking the den!" gasped Danny. "It's enormous! It climbed on the roof and…"

Rosie started to giggle. "What's so funny?" demanded Danny.

"It's only Archie," Rosie laughed, pointing. "He's eaten a great big hole in the roof." Danny looked around and began to laugh as well. "Aah, Archie," Rosie sighed, "did you want to join in our adventure too?"

"Come on, Rosie," said Danny. "Let's fix the den. But this time we'll leave a little window at the back so that Archie doesn't have to eat the roof to join in!"

Where's Wanda?

Sally was worried. Wanda, her cat, was getting fat. She was behaving very strangely, too. She wouldn't go in her basket. "She must be ill," Sally told her mummy. "Her tummy's all swollen, and she hasn't slept in her basket for days."

"Don't worry," said Mummy, giving Sally a hug. "If she's not better in the morning, we'll take her to the vet."

"Sssh!" whispered Sally. "You know how much Wanda hates the V-E-T." But it was too late, Wanda had already gone.

Sally and her mummy couldn't find Wanda anywhere. She didn't even come running when they left out a saucer of milk. Wanda was still missing the following morning.

"She must have heard us talking about the vet," said Sally, as they searched around the house. "Perhaps she's hiding in the garden," she said.

They looked in the flowerbed, under the hedge, and up the tree. But all they found there were the birds. "Sometimes she sunbathes in the vegetable patch," said Sally. But the only animal there was a fluffy rabbit.

"Wanda!" called Mummy, looking in the shed. Wanda often liked sleeping in there. Today all they found there were mice.

"Maybe she's been locked in the garage," said Sally.

They looked around the car. They looked in the car. They even looked under it. But all they found there were spiders.

Wanda was nowhere around the house or garden, so Mummy took Sally to look in the park. "Here, Wanda!" called Sally. But all they found there were dogs. Wanda hated dogs, so she wouldn't be there.

On the way home, Sally even sat on Mummy's shoulders so that she could look on top of people's garages and sheds. "She must have run away," cried Sally. "We're never going to find her."

But Mummy had an idea. She helped Sally to draw some pictures of Wanda. Then they wrote MISSING and their telephone number on the pictures. They posted the leaflets through all the letterboxes in the street.

In the afternoon Mrs Jones from next door popped her head over the hedge. "Come and see what I've found in my laundry basket," smiled Mrs Jones. Sally and her mummy rushed next door at once. When Sally saw what Mrs Jones had in her laundry basket she couldn't believe her eyes.

There, sitting amongst the washing, was Wanda. She looked very slim and very proud. And beside her lay five tiny kittens. They were so young that their eyes were still closed. Wanda hadn't been ill after all. She'd been expecting kittens!

Mrs Jones said that they could keep the basket until Wanda had finished with it. So Mummy carried the new family home as Sally skipped beside her.

Sally was so excited. She just couldn't wait to tell people how they'd gone searching for one cat and found six!

The Mean King and the Crafty Lad

There was once a king who was as mean as he was rich. He lived in a great palace where he spent his days counting his bags of gold coins. Meanwhile his subjects lived in great poverty. Sometimes the king would summon his page to prepare the royal carriage. Then the king would set forth in his great, golden coach to survey his kingdom.

Now not only was the king extremely rich, but he was also very vain. As he passed his subjects working in the field, he liked them to bow to him and pay him compliments. "How handsome you look today, Your Majesty!" they would call, or "How well the colour pink suits you, Sire!"

His head would swell with pride as he moved on. "My people truly adore me!" he would say.

But, for all their complimentary words, the people hated their king. They resented the fact that the king lived in splendour while his subjects toiled hard all their lives. At last a secret meeting was called among the peasants. "Let's sign a petition demanding our rights!" cried one man.

"And fair pay!" shouted another. They all cheered and clapped their hands.

"Who's going to write down our demands?" called an old woman. Now the crowd was hushed, for none of them knew how to read or write.

"I know what we can do instead," called a voice from the back. Everyone turned round to see a young lad in rags. "Let's march on the palace!" he cried.

"Yes!" roared the crowd.

As the angry mob reached the palace, the king saw them and sent out his guard dogs. The peasants were forced to flee for their lives with the dogs snapping at their ankles. Not until the last peasant was out of sight did the king call off his dogs.

"Good work!" he cried. From then on, however, life became even harder for the people because the king was on his guard in case they marched on the castle again. Now, when he went out and about in his kingdom, he was always accompanied by his hounds.

Eventually, another secret meeting was called. "What can we do?" the people said. "We will never be able to get past those savage dogs."

"I've got an idea," came a familiar voice. It was the ragged lad again. For a while there was uproar as folk accused him of having nearly lost them their lives. "Please trust me," pleaded the lad. "I know I let you down, but this time I've got a well thought-out plan to get the king to give up his money."

In the end, the peasants listened to the boy's scheme and they decided to let him try.

The next day, the boy hid in a branch of a tree that overhung the palace garden. With him he had some dog biscuits, in which he had hidden a powerful sleeping pill. He threw the biscuits on to the palace lawn and waited. Some time later, as the boy had hoped, the king's hounds came out on to the lawn. They headed straight for the biscuits and gobbled them up. Soon they were fast asleep, one and all.

Quickly the lad slid out of the tree and, donning a large black cape, he ran round to the front of the palace and rapped on the door. A sentry opened the door. "Good day," said the lad, "I am Victor, the world-famous vet. Do you have any animals requiring medical attention?"

"No," replied the sentry, slamming the door in the lad's face. Just then voices could be heard from within the palace and the sentry opened the door again saying, "Actually, we do have a problem. Step inside."

The sentry led the lad out to the lawn where the king was weeping over the dogs' bodies. "Oh, please help," he cried. "I need my dogs. Without them I may be besieged by my own people."

The lad pretended to examine the dogs. He said to the king, "I have seen one case like this. The only cure is to feed the animals liquid gold."

"Liquid gold?" exclaimed the king. "Where shall I find it?"

"Fear not," said the lad, "I have a friend – a witch – who lives in the mountains. She can turn gold coins into liquid gold. If you let me take all the dogs to her she will cure them. But you will have to give me a bag of gold to take to her."

Well, the king was so worried that he readily agreed. The sleeping dogs were loaded on to a horse-drawn cart, and the king gave the lad a bag of gold saying, "Hurry back, my dogs are most precious."

The lad went home. His parents helped him unload the dogs, who by now were beginning to wake up. They took great care of the dogs and the next day the lad put on the cloak again and returned to the palace.

"The good news is," he said to the king, "that the cure is working. The bad news is that there was only enough gold to revive one dog. I'll need all the gold you've got to cure the others."

"Take it all," screamed the king, "only I must have my dogs back tomorrow!" He opened the safe and threw his entire stock of gold on to another cart, which the young lad dragged away.

That night the lad gave each of the king's subjects a bag of gold. The next morning he led the dogs back to the palace. To his surprise, the king didn't want them back. "Now I have no gold," he said, "I don't need guard dogs."

Then the lad saw that the king had learned his lesson, and he told the king what had really happened. And, to everyone's joy, the king said the peasants could keep their bags of gold. As for the king, he kept the dogs as pets and became a much nicer person.

No One Like You

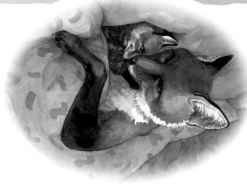

Ruff was hungry. A huge grumble rumbled round his tummy. He could hear Rufus clattering round in the kitchen. A delicious smell of freshly baked cakes sailed past his nose.

"Yummy," thought Ruff.

Ruff skipped into the kitchen – Rufus was washing up while the cakes cooled down.

"Would you like some help?" asked Ruff. "I could try one of those cakes for you."

"Oh, really!" said Rufus, smiling.

"No one makes cakes like you," said Ruff.

Ruff was bored. He twiddled his fingers, tapped his toes and twiddled his fingers again. He had no one to play with.

Later, Ruff tiptoed back into the living room – Rufus was reading.

"Would you like something better to read?" asked Ruff. "I could find you an exciting story."

"Oh, really!" said Rufus, smiling.

"No one tells a story like you," said Ruff.

Ruff was fed up. He was trying to make a model car. He fiddled and twiddled and fiddled, but he couldn't put it together.

Then he had an idea! Ruff galloped into the garden – Rufus was digging.

"Would you like something fun to do?" asked Ruff. "I could let you help me with my model car."

"Oh, really!" said Rufus, smiling.

"No one's as much fun as you," said Ruff.

It was bedtime! Rufus tucked Ruff into bed.

Ruff was feeling scared.
He didn't like the shadows that flickered all round – it was very quiet. Then he had an idea! Ruff crept out of his bedroom and into Rufus' room.

Rufus was snoring loudly. It made Ruff giggle, which woke Rufus up.

"Would you like someone to cuddle?" asked Ruff.
"I'm very good at cuddling."

"Oh, really!" said Rufus, smiling.

"No one cuddles like you," yawned Ruff, and he climbed into Rufus' bed.

"Oh, really!" said Rufus…
"Well, no one loves you as much as I do, because there's no one like you."

There Was a Man, and His Name Was Dob

There was a man, and his name was Dob,
    And he had a wife, and her name was Mob,
And he had a dog, and he called it Cob,
    And she had a cat, called Chitterabob.
Cob, says Dob,
    Chitterabob, says Mob,
Cob was Dob's dog,
    Chitterabob Mob's cat.

Me, Myself, and I

Me, myself, and I –
    We went to the kitchen and ate a pie.
Then my mother she came in
    And chased us out with a rolling pin.

Swan Swam Over the Sea

Swan swam over the sea –
    Swim, swan, swim,
Swan swam back again,
    Well swum swan.

Hey, Dorolot, Dorolot!

    Hey, dorolot, dorolot!
      Hey, dorolay, dorolay!
    Hey, my bonny boat, bonny boat,
      Hey, drag away, drag away!

My Grandmother Sent Me

My grandmother sent me a new-fashioned three-cornered
cambric country-cut handkerchief. Not an old-fashioned
three-cornered cambric country-cut handkerchief, but
a new-fashioned three-cornered cambric country-
cut handkerchief.

Adam and Eve and Pinchme

Adam and Eve and Pinchme
   Went down to the river to bathe.
Adam and Eve were drowned –
   Who do you think was saved?

Peter Piper

Peter Piper picked a peck of pickled pepper;
   A peck of pickled pepper Peter Piper picked;
If Peter Piper picked a peck of pickled pepper,
   Where's the peck of pickled pepper Peter Piper picked?

Robert Rowley

Robert Rowley rolled a round roll round,
   A round roll Robert Rowley rolled round;
Where rolled the round roll Robert Rowley rolled round?

Peter Meets a Dragon

Once upon a time there was a young boy named Peter. He lived in an ordinary house with an ordinary Mum and Dad, an ordinary sister and an ordinary pet cat, called Jasper. In fact, everything in Peter's life was so ordinary that he sometimes wished that something extraordinary would happen. "Why doesn't a giant come and squash the house flat with his foot?" he wondered. But, each day, Peter would wake up in the morning and everything was just the same as it had been the day before.

One morning when Peter woke up there was a very strange smell in the house. Looking out of his bedroom window, he saw that the front lawn was scorched and blackened. There was smoke drifting off the grass and, further away, he could see some bushes ablaze.

Peter rushed downstairs and out of the front door. He ran out of the garden and down the lane following the trail of smoke and burning grass. He grew more and more puzzled, however, as there was no sign of anything that could have caused such a blaze.

Peter was about to run home and tell his Mum and Dad, when he heard a panting noise coming from the undergrowth. Parting the bushes, he found a young creature with green, scaly skin, a pair of wings and a long snout full of sharp teeth. Every now and again a little tongue of flames came from its nostrils, setting the grass around it on fire. "A baby dragon!" Peter said to himself, in great surprise. Big tears were rolling out of the dragon's yellow eyes and down its scaly cheeks as it flapped its wings desperately and tried to take off.

When the dragon saw Peter it stopped flapping its wings. "Oh, woe is me!" it sobbed. "Where am I?"

"Where do you want to be?" asked Peter, kneeling down on the scorched ground.

"I want to be in Dragonland with my friends," replied the dragon. "We were all flying together, but I got tired and needed a rest. I called to the others but they didn't hear me. I just had to stop and get my breath back. Now I don't know where I am, or if I'll ever see my friends again!"

"I'm sure I can help you get home," said Peter, but he had no idea how.

"You?" hissed a voice. "How could you possibly help? You're just a boy!" Peter looked round, and to his astonishment found Jasper sitting behind him. "I suppose you're going to wave a magic wand, are you?" continued Jasper. "You need to call in an expert."

Then he turned his back on Peter and the baby dragon and started washing his paws.

Peter was astounded. He'd never heard Jasper talking before. "W… w… what do you mean?" he stammered.

"Well," said Jasper, glancing over his shoulder at Peter, "I reckon that horse over there could help. Follow me."

Jasper leaped up on to the gate and called to the horse. Then he whispered in the horse's ear. The horse whispered back in Jasper's ear. "He's got a friend on the other side of the wood who'll help," said Jasper.

"But how?" said Peter, looking perplexed.

"Be patient! Follow me!" said Jasper as he stalked off through the grass. "And tell your friend to stop setting fire to everything!" he added.

"I can't help it," cried Flame, about to burst into tears again. "Every time I get out of breath I start to pant, and then I start breathing fire."

"Let me carry you," said Peter. He picked up Flame in his arms and ran after Jasper. The baby dragon felt very strange. He was cold and clammy, but his mouth was breathing hot smoke, which made Peter's eyes water. He followed Jasper's upright tail through the wood to a field, and in the field was a horse. But this was no ordinary horse. Peter stopped dead in his tracks and stared. The horse was pure milky white, and from its head grew a single, long horn. "A unicorn!" breathed Peter.

Jasper was talking to the unicorn. He beckoned with his paw to Peter.

"He'll take you both to his home, Peter." And with that, Jasper was off.

"Climb aboard," said the unicorn gently.

Peter and the little dragon scrambled up on to the unicorn's back. "What an adventure," thought Peter as they soared through the clouds. He saw a mountain ahead, then they descended through the clouds and landed right at the top of the mountain. "I'm home!" squeaked Flame joyously as they landed. Sure enough, several dragons were running over to greet him. They looked quite friendly, but some of them were rather large and one was breathing a great deal of fire.

"Time for me to go," said Peter a little nervously, as Flame jumped off the unicorn's back and flew to the ground. The unicorn took off again and soon they were back in the field once more. When Peter turned to thank the unicorn he saw that it was just an ordinary horse with no trace of a horn at all. Peter walked back home across the field, but there was no sign of burnt grass and his lawn was in perfect condition too. Peter felt rather perplexed. "I hope Jasper can explain," he thought, as the cat ran past him and into the house. "Jasper, what's happened to the burnt grass?" he blurted out. But Jasper didn't say a word, he ignored Peter and curled up in his basket.

When Peter wasn't looking, however, Jasper gave him a glance that said, "Well, was that a big enough adventure for you?"

Sniffle

A long way away, in a jungle no one had ever been to before, lived the Sniffle monster.

The famous explorer, Major Jolly, went into the jungle looking for new animals. First, he found a big, bright bird that strutted about showing everyone what a great tail it had. Then he found a new type of monkey that could knit socks! His greatest discovery, though, was when he came upon the MONSTER, in a tree, eating a banana. Major Jolly got very excited, the monster was intelligent! That means it could think like you and me. The monster was quite ugly, but then he would be, wouldn't he? He was big, ugly and covered in red fur.

Major Jolly decided to take him home to show his wife. They flew back together in a big plane and the monster sat on three seats. The famous explorer's wife met them at the airport.

"This is the monster I discovered, Maud," said Major Jolly. "How do you do?" Maud held out her hand.

"Howdeedoodee," repeated the monster. He took the lady's hand and sniffed it, and then danced her round the room in circles.

"I've already started to teach him English," said Maud, as they danced past for the third time.

Back home the monster wanted to dance with

everyone at first! But just a few weeks later he began to look ill and sad.
He coughed and sniffed and spluttered. His coat turned green, and
patches of fur fell out. And he had something really nasty running out of
his nose.

When Maud visited, he wouldn't dance round the
room with her. "My dear Monster," she said,
"what's wrong with you?"

"I am Sniffle monster!" he said. "I was taken
away from jungle without my friend. I must have
this friend with me always, or I get ill! Stuff comes
out of my nose! My friend is Hanky monster."

Maud thought she understood. "And you need this Hanky monster...
umm... to wipe your nose for you?"

"No, no, no!" said Sniffle. "Hanky is a magician. He will make Sniffle
dance again! Only Hanky monster knows the secret magic potion."

Major Jolly took Sniffle back to the jungle to find the Hanky monster.
They found the place in the jungle where Major Jolly had camped.
Suddenly, something that looked like a giant cabbage appeared and
threw itself at Sniffle. Sniffle gave a whoop of joy! The cabbage was the
Hanky monster, of course! It rushed back into the jungle.

"Gone to get magic potion," whispered Sniffle weakly.

The Hanky monster came back with a drink in a coconut shell. Sniffle
drank it and went straight to bed. Next morning his colour was back to
red and his nose had stopped running. He danced
with everyone. Major Jolly was desperate
to know the secret of the magic drink.

Hanky monster winked and
whispered, "Hot lemon and honey!"

You Can Do It, Dilly Duck!

It was the night before Dilly's first swimming lesson.

"I've got a funny feeling in my tummy," said Dilly, as Mamma Duck kissed her goodnight.

"Don't worry!" replied her mother. "Just close your eyes tightly and you'll soon fall asleep." Dilly shut her eyes and tried to go to sleep. But all she could think about was the lesson.

"What if I sink?" she worried. Dilly pictured Mamma Duck's smiling face. "If Mamma Duck can float, perhaps I can, too," she thought. Then she snuggled down to go to sleep.

Suddenly Dilly opened her eyes. "But I'll get all wet!" she quacked, shaking her feathers. Dilly thought about her friend Webster the frog. "Webster loves getting wet," she remembered. "He says it's fun!"

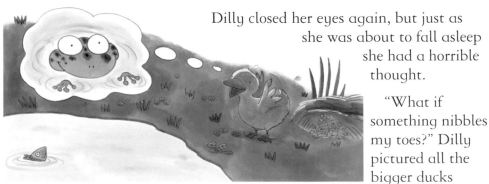

Dilly closed her eyes again, but just as she was about to fall asleep she had a horrible thought.

"What if something nibbles my toes?" Dilly pictured all the bigger ducks

You Can Do It, Dilly Duck!

doing duck-dives in the pond. "They're not afraid of what's under the water," she quacked, "so why should I be?" Dilly was wide awake early the next morning, and so were all her friends.

"You can do it, Dilly!" they cheered as she waddled slowly to the edge of the pond. She leaned forward and looked in, very timidly. There in the water was another little duckling gazing back at her. Dilly looked at the other little duckling. She was small and yellow with downy feathers, just like Dilly.

"Well, if you can do it, I guess I can too!" quacked Dilly bravely. SPLASH! She jumped right into the pond. "I can float!" cried Dilly, paddling along. "It's fun getting wet!" Then Dilly did a duck-dive.

"There's nothing scary under the water either!" she added, bobbing up again. "In fact, you are all right! I CAN do it!"

Tiger Tales

Louis and Lisa Lion were just learning to pounce, and their dad had told them to practise as much as they could. So they were prowling through the jungle, looking for prey to pounce upon.

"There's something orange and blue and fluttery," whispered Lisa. "Here I go…" As Lisa pounced on the butterfly, Louis spotted something green and jumpy. He crept up and… POUNCED! As the two little cubs bounded through the jungle, Louis suddenly saw a flash of orange and black in some bushes.

"A stripy snake!" he whispered. "It's too good to pass up!" So, at just the right moment, he… POUNCED!

"Owwww!" came a voice from the bush. "What's got my tail?" The snake turned out to be attached to a stripy cub, just the same size as Louis and Lisa.

"Who are you?" they asked.

"I'm Timmy Tiger," said the little cub. "I've just moved here from The Other Side of the Jungle!"

"We're Louis and Lisa Lion," said Lisa. "Why don't we show you our side of the jungle?"

"Here's our river," said Louis proudly.

"It's nice," said Timmy, "but it's kind of small. Our river on The Other

Side of the Jungle is as wide as fifty tall palm trees laid end to end! And I can swim across that river – and back – without stopping once!"

"We can't even swim," said Lisa. "Will you show us how?"

"Err… maybe another time," said Timmy. "I'm just getting over the sniffles, and Mum said I shouldn't swim for a while."

A little farther along, Louis and Lisa saw Howard Hippo wallowing merrily in the mud.

"Meet our new friend, Timmy Tiger!" they called.

Howard opened his mouth in a big grin. "Nice to meet you!" he called.

"Er… same here," said Timmy, keeping his distance.

As the cubs scampered on, Timmy said, "On The Other Side of the Jungle, there's a hippo with a mouth as big as a cave. Three tigers can sit in it!"

As the cubs walked on, something from a branch above dropped down in front of them. Timmy jumped, but Louis and Lisa smiled. "Hi, Seymour! Meet our new friend, Timmy Tiger."

"Greetingsssss," hissed Seymour Snake. "Niccce to make your aquaintancccccce!"

"Nice to meet you, too," said Timmy, a little uncertainly. "Well, ssso long," said Seymour, as he slithered off. "Sssssee you sssssoon I ssupposse!"

As Seymour slithered off, Timmy said, "On The Other Side of the Jungle, there are snakes as thick as tree trunks. Once, one of them swallowed me!"

"Oh, no!" cried Louis and Lisa.

"Yes," Timmy said, "but my dad hit the snake on the head and made him spit me out! My dad's really, really strong, and he's twice as big as an elephant, and he can carry six gorillas on his back! And my mum can stand on her front paws and juggle coconuts with her hind legs, and… "

"…and what?" asked two smiling, normal-sized tigers on the path in front of them.

"…and, here they are," said Timmy, sheepishly. "Mum and Dad, meet my friends, Louis and Lisa."

"Happy to meet you," said Mr and Mrs Tiger.

"As you can see," Mrs Tiger added, "we are very ordinary and normal tigers."

"But what about all those amazing things Timmy told us?" asked Louis. "What about The Other Side of the Jungle?"

"It's just like this side," said Mr Tiger.

"So the river isn't as wide as fifty palm trees?" asked Lisa.

"And there's no hippo with a mouth as big as a cave, or a snake who swallowed Timmy?" asked Louis.

"No, indeed!" laughed Mrs Tiger. Timmy looked embarrassed. "Well, they were good stories," he said.

"Yes," said Mrs Tiger, "but they were just stories." She turned to Louis and Lisa. "Timmy had no friends to play with in our old home, he spent his time imagining amazing adventures."

"But now that he's got friends like you two to play with," said Mr Tiger, "perhaps he'll have some real adventures!"

"And there are more friends to meet, Timmy," Lisa said, "like Mickey and Maxine Monkey, and Chico Chimp!"

"You know, there are monkeys and chimps on The Other Side of the Jungle, too," said Timmy.

"Really?" said Lisa, glancing at her brother.

"Yes," said Timmy, "but I didn't know them. I can't wait to meet Mickey, Maxine and Chico!"

"Well, what are we waiting for?" said Louis, and they all raced off, ready for fun and excitement on This Side of the Jungle.

Chasing Tails

Barney had been chasing his tail all morning. Round and round he went, until he made himself feel quite dizzy.

"Can't you find something useful to do?" asked the cat, from where she sat watching him on the fence.

"What? Like chasing lazy cats?" said Barney, as he leapt towards her, barking fiercely.

Later, as he trotted around the farmyard, Barney thought about what the cat had said. He wished he could be more useful, but he was only a little pup. When he grew up, he would be a fine, useful farm dog, like his mum. Just then, he rounded the barn, and there in front of him waved a big bushy tail…

"Here's a tail I can catch!" thought Barney playfully, and he sprang forward and sank his sharp little puppy teeth into it!

Now, the tail belonged to a sly fox, who was about to pounce on Mrs Hen and her chicks! The fox yelped in surprise, and ran away across the fields.

"Ooh, Barney, you saved us!" cried Mrs Hen.

The cat was watching from the fence. "Maybe all that practice chasing tails has come in useful after all!" she said.

Hannah Bantry

Hannah Bantry,
    In the pantry,
Gnawing on a mutton bone;
    How she gnawed it,
    How she clawed it,
When she found herself alone.

Eeper Weeper

Eeper Weeper, Chimney sweeper,
Married a wife and could not keep her.
    Married another,
    Did not love her,
Up the chimney he did shove her!

Go to Bed

Go to bed late,
    Stay very small;
Go to bed early
    Grow very tall.

Sippity, Sippity Sup

Sippity sup, sippity sup,
    Bread and milk from a china cup.
Bread and milk from a bright silver spoon
    Made of a piece of the bright silver moon.
Sippity sup, sippity sup,
    Sippity, sippity sup.

Where Am I?

X, Y, and tumbledown Z,
The cat's in the cupboard
And can't see me!

Little Blue Ben

Little Blue Ben, who lives in the glen,
Keeps a blue cat and one blue hen,
Which lays of blue eggs a score and ten;
Where shall I find the little Blue Ben?

Dame Trot

Dame Trot and her cat
    Sat down for a chat;
The dame sat on this side
    And puss sat on that.

"Puss," says the dame,
    "Can you catch a rat,
Or a mouse in the dark?"
    "Purr," says the cat.

I Do Not Like Thee

I do not like thee, Doctor Fell,
    The reason why, I cannot tell;
But this I know, and know full well,
    I do not like thee, Doctor Fell.

Sunshine

A sunshiny shower
    Won't last half an hour.

Old Bandy Legs

As I was going to sell my eggs,
    I met a man with bandy legs;
Bandy legs and crooked toes,
    I tripped up his heels and
        he fell on his nose.

My Mummy's Maid

Dingty diddlety,
    My mummy's maid,
She stole oranges,
    I am afraid;
Some in her pocket,
    Some in her sleeve,
She stole oranges,
    I do believe.

One, Two

One, two, whatever you do,
    Start it well and carry it through.
Try, try, never say die,
    Things will come right,
You know, by and by.

One Little Indian

One little, two little, three little Indians,
Four little, five little, six little Indians,
Seven little, eight little, nine little Indians,
Ten little Indian boys.

Ten little, nine little, eight little Indians,
Seven little, six little, five little Indians,
Four little, three little, two little Indians,
One little Indian boy.

Charlie Wag

Charlie Wag,
    Charlie Wag,
Ate the pudding
    And left the bag.

Bear Finds a Friend

Sally found the teddy bear in the park. She might not have noticed it, but her ball rolled under a bush and she had crawled beneath it to get it back. It was a small, light brown bear, wearing pale blue dungarees and a red and white striped shirt. "Look, Mum," said Sally, "Someone's left their teddy here. What shall we do with it?"

"We'd better take it home with us," said Mum. "We'll put a notice up to say we found it." Sally made a notice and Mum helped her to spell the words, "Teddy bear found. Please ring this number." Sally wrote her telephone number. Then she brushed the leaves from the bear and sat it next to her own teddy. She put her teddy's arm round it. "Look after him," she told her teddy. "He must be feeling very frightened."

Sally and Mum took the notice to the park, and pinned it to a tree near the playground. "Now we'll have to wait and see," said Mum.

The telephone rang just before tea time. "Yes, you can come and get it straight away," Mum said. She turned to Sally. "The little girl who lost the teddy bear is coming to fetch it." The doorbell rang and a small girl was standing on the step with her mother. She smiled at Sally, "Thank you for looking after my teddy," she said.

"He made friends with my teddy," said Sally. The girl picked up her bear and hugged him tight.

"Perhaps we could be friends, too," she said.

318

Bear's Picnic

In a sunny clearing in the wood, Ellie, her brother Alex, and Ellie's teddy bear were playing hide and seek. "Sit quietly," said Ellie to her teddy, as she placed him carefully behind a tree. "Alex won't find you there." Then she ran off to hide.

"Time to pack up the picnic things," called Ellie's mother. "We need to hurry before it starts to rain." Ellie and Alex collected the plates and cups.

"Race you back to the car," yelled Alex, charging off through the trees.

"I can beat you!" cried Ellie, following. But no one thought of Teddy.

Teddy sat under the tree. A huge leaf drifted down, and landed in front of him. A squirrel hopped along the branch above, dropping the nut he was carrying, and it plopped down onto the leaf in front of the bear. High above, a bird flew past, carrying a blackberry. The blackberry slipped from its beak and fell down onto the leaf, too.

"We've forgotten Teddy!" screamed Ellie in the car. As she and Alex ran through the trees, they startled a mouse, who'd stopped to look at the strange creature sitting under the tree. The mouse opened his mouth to squeak and dropped a seed onto the leaf at the furry creature's feet.

"Look," said Ellie, peering round the tree. "Here he is. He stayed behind to eat his own picnic." She hugged her teddy bear tightly.

"We'll take your plate home with us," she smiled, picking up the leaf.

The
Sad Clown

Bongo the clown had a bit of a problem. Clowns were supposed to be happy, funny, jolly people, but Bongo was a very sad clown. Nothing at all seemed to make him laugh.

Whenever the circus came to town people from all around flocked to the big top hoping for an exciting day out. They thrilled to the daring performance of the high-wire act, as the acrobats leaped from one swinging trapeze to the next. They enjoyed the jugglers, who tossed bright, sparkling balls into the air while standing on one leg. And the crowd delighted in seeing the beautiful white horses parading around the circus ring with the bareback riders balancing on their backs. When the seals came on, there was always a big cheer from the crowd, for everyone loved them and could watch their clever antics for hours.

But the biggest favourite of the crowd, especially with all the children, was the clown. Everyone laughed to see him dressed in his big baggy trousers and with his funny walk. They laughed even more when they saw his big floppy hat with the revolving flower on it. Even his painted clown face made them laugh.

But, when his act started, the crowd thought they would burst with laughter. First of all his bicycle fell apart as he tried to ride around the ring. Then he fell out of his motor car when the seat tipped up. By the time he had accidentally poured cold water down his trousers and fallen into the custard-filled swimming pool, the crowd were almost crying with laughter.

But, beneath all the make up, Bongo the sad clown wasn't smiling at all. In fact, he saw nothing funny at all in bicycles that fell apart as you used them, or cars that tipped you out as you went along, or having cold water poured down your trousers, or even ending up face first in a swimming pool full of custard. He simply hadn't got a sense of humour.

All the other performers in the circus decided they would try to cheer up the sad clown.

"I know," said the high-wire trapeze acrobat, "let's paint an even funnier face on him. That'll make him laugh."

So that's what they did, but Bongo still didn't laugh and was still just as sad.

"Let us perform some of our tricks, just for him," said the seals.

So they sat on their stools and tossed their big coloured balls to each other, clapped their flippers together and made lots of honking sounds. But Bongo still didn't laugh. In fact, nothing that anyone tried made poor Bongo smile. He was still a very sad clown.

Then Percival the ringmaster spoke. "You know, I think I know what the problem is," he said. "There is nothing a clown likes better than playing tricks on other clowns. Perhaps, if we had a second clown, that would cheer up Bongo."

So right away they hired another clown, called Piffle.

The circus arrived in the next town and soon it was time for Bongo and Piffle's act. Piffle started riding around on his bike while Bongo pretended to wash the car by throwing a bucket of water over it. Instead of the water landing on the car, of course, it went all over Piffle, who just happened to be cycling past at that moment. A little smile flickered across Bongo's face at the sight of the soaking wet Piffle.

Next, Bongo and Piffle pretended to be cooking, and Bongo tripped while carrying two huge custard pies. Both landed right in Piffle's face. Bongo let out a huge chuckle of laughter when he saw Piffle's face covered in custard.

At the end of their act, the clowns were pretending to be decorators, painting up a ladder. Of course, you've guessed it. The ladders fell down and all the pots of paint landed on the two clowns. Bongo looked across at Piffle, who had a big paint pot stuck on his head, with paint dripping down his body. Bongo threw back his head and roared with laughter. Piffle thought Bongo looked just as funny with paint all over his body, too. And as for the crowd – well, they thought two clowns were even funnier than one and they clapped and cheered and filled the big top with laughter.

After that Bongo was never a sad clown again.

Cheeky Chick

Cheeky Chick was a playful little chick. He was always playing tricks on his brothers and sisters. He would hide in the long grass, then jump out on them in surprise, shouting, "Boo!" One day they decided to get their own back. "Let's play hide and seek," they said.

They left Cheeky Chick to count to ten, while they all went to hide. Cheeky Chick hunted high and low for his brothers and sisters. He looked in all his favourite hiding places but they were nowhere to be found.

"Come out," he called. "I give up!" But no one came.

So Cheeky Chick carried on looking. He searched carefully all through the farmyard, through the vegetable patch and in all the empty flower pots. He searched along the hedgerow at the edge of the field. He even looked in the haystack, which took a very long time, but there was

no sign of his brothers and sisters to be found amongst the hay.

By now it was getting dark, and Cheeky Chick was feeling scared and lonely. "It's no use," he said to himself. "I'll have to go home."

He hurried to the hen house and opened the door. "Surprise!" came a loud chorus. His brothers and sisters had been hiding there all along! It was a long time before Cheeky Chick played tricks on them again.

The Boy Who Wished Too Much

There once was a young boy named Billy. He was a lucky lad, for he had parents who loved him, plenty of friends and a room full of toys. Behind his house was a rubbish tip. Billy had been forbidden to go there by his mother, but he used to stare at it out of the window. It looked such an exciting place to explore.

One day, Billy was staring at the rubbish tip, when he saw something gold-coloured gleaming in the sunlight. There, on the top of the tip, sat a brass lamp. Now Billy knew the tale of Aladdin, and he wondered if this lamp could possibly be magic, too. When his mother wasn't looking he slipped out of the back door, scrambled up the tip and snatched the lamp from the top.

Billy ran to the garden shed. It was quite dark inside, but Billy could see the brass of the lamp glowing softly in his hands. When his eyes had grown accustomed to the dark, he saw that the lamp was quite dirty. As he started to rub at the brass, there was a puff of smoke and the shed was filled with light. Billy closed his eyes tightly and, when he opened them again, he found to his astonishment that there was a man standing there, dressed in a costume richly embroidered with gold and jewels. "I am the genie of the lamp," he said. "Are you by any chance Aladdin?"

"N… n… no, I'm Billy," stammered Billy, staring in disbelief.

"How very confusing," said the genie frowning. "I was told that the boy with the lamp was named Aladdin. Oh well! Now I'm here, I may as well grant you your wishes. You can have three, by the way."

At first Billy was so astonished he couldn't speak. Then he began to think hard. What would be the very best thing to wish for? He had an idea. "My first wish," he said, "is that I can have as many wishes as I want."

The genie looked rather taken aback, but then he smiled and said, "A wish is a wish. So be it!"

Billy could hardly believe his ears. Was he really going to get all his wishes granted? He decided to start with a really big wish, just in case the genie changed his mind later. "I wish I could have a purse that never runs out of money," he said.

Hey presto! There in his hand was a purse with five coins in it. Without remembering to thank the genie, Billy ran out of the shed and down the road to the sweet shop. He bought a large bag of sweets and took one of the coins out of his purse to pay for it. Then he peeped cautiously inside the purse, and sure enough there were still five coins. The magic had worked! Billy ran back to the garden shed to get his next wish, but the genie had vanished.

"That's not fair!" cried Billy, stamping his foot. Then he remembered the lamp. He seized it and rubbed at it furiously. Sure enough, the genie reappeared.

"Don't forget to share those sweets with your friends," he said. "What is your wish, Billy?"

This time Billy, who was very fond of sweet things, said, "I wish I had a house made of chocolate!"

No sooner had he uttered the words than he found that he was standing outside a house made entirely of rich, creamy chocolate. Billy broke off the door knocker and nibbled at it. Yes, it really was made of delicious chocolate! Billy gorged himself until he felt sick. He lay down on the grass and closed his eyes. When he opened them again, the chocolate house had vanished and he was outside the garden shed once more. "It's not fair to take my chocolate house away. I want it back!" he complained, stamping his foot once again.

Billy went back into the shed. "This time I'll ask for something that lasts longer," he thought. He rubbed the lamp and there stood the genie again.

This time Billy wished for a magic carpet to take him to faraway lands. No sooner were the words out of his mouth than he could feel himself being lifted up and out of the shed on a lovely soft carpet. The carpet took Billy up, up and away over hills, mountains and seas to the ends of the Earth. He saw camels in the desert, polar bears at the North Pole and whales far

out at sea. At last, Billy
began to feel homesick
and he asked the
magic carpet to take
him home.

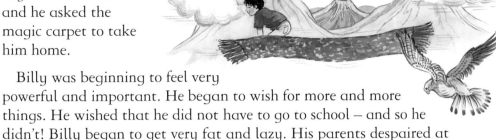

Billy was beginning to feel very
powerful and important. He began to wish for more and more
things. He wished that he did not have to go to school – and so he
didn't! Billy began to get very fat and lazy. His parents despaired at
how spoiled he had become. His friends no longer came to play because
he had grown so boastful.

One morning, Billy woke up and burst into tears. "I'm so lonely and
unhappy!" he wailed. He realised that there was only one thing to do.
He ran down to the garden shed, picked up the lamp and rubbed it.

"You don't look very happy," said the genie, giving him a concerned
glance. "What is your wish?"

"I wish everything was back to normal," Billy blurted out, "and I wish
I could have no more wishes!"

"A wise choice!" said the genie. "So be it. Goodbye, Billy!" And with
that the genie vanished. Billy stepped out of the shed, and from then on
everything was normal again. His parents cared for him, he went to
school and his friends came to play once more. But Billy had learned

his lesson.
He never
boasted
again and
he always
shared his
sweets and
all his toys.

Ebby, the Smallest Pup

Ebby was the smallest puppy in the litter. His brothers and sisters were all bigger than he was. He wouldn't have minded, but they were always teasing him.

"Out the way, titch!" they laughed, as they pushed him to the side at meal times.

"Last one's a baby," they barked, as they rushed out to play. And, of course, Ebby lost every time.

"You're small because you were the last to be born," explained his mum. "And that's why you're so special." But Ebby didn't feel very special. In fact, he just felt sad.

One day, a family came to see the puppies. "Look smart," said their mother. "They've come to take one of you home."

Of course, all the puppies wanted to be chosen but only one could go – and it wasn't Ebby.

After that, lots of people came to the house. Each of them left with a puppy of their own, but nobody chose Ebby. Eventually, Ebby was the only puppy left.

"Nobody wants me," sniffed Ebby. "I'm not as good as other dogs."

"Don't be silly," said his mum. "You're just special, you'll see."

EBBY, THE SMALLEST PUP

The next day, a little girl came to the house. "Oh, goody! They saved him for me," she laughed.

Ebby looked around to see who she was talking about. But, of course, nobody else was there.

Suddenly, Ebby was lifted into the air and whirled around. "You are the cutest puppy in the whole wide world!" smiled the little girl.

Ebby felt a bit giddy but he smiled back anyway. It seemed that somebody did want him, after all.

"I wonder where we're going," thought Ebby, as he waved goodbye to his mum. But he soon found out because his new home was just next door!

When Ebby was old enough, Helen and her daddy took him for a walk in the woods, and he was very pleased when his mum came too. There were other dogs walking in the woods and Ebby felt shy. He hid behind his mum. He didn't want everyone to see how small he was.

Suddenly, something small and soft hurtled into him. "Hiya, titch!" barked a familiar voice. It was his biggest brother, but he seemed to have shrunk. He was only as high as Ebby's shoulder.

"He hasn't shrunk," laughed his mum, when Ebby whispered in her ear. "You've grown, silly. It's all that food Helen gives you."

After that, Ebby and his brother had great fun playing together. They had even more fun when they were joined by two of their sisters.

Their mum watched proudly as they raced around the trees. And she couldn't help smiling when Ebby turned around and barked, "Last one's a baby!"

The Grand Old Duke of York

The grand old Duke of York,
  He had ten thousand men;
He marched them up to the top of the hill,
  And he marched them down again!

And when they were up they were up,
  And when they were down they were down;
And when they were only halfway up,
  They were neither up nor down.

What is the Rhyme for Porringer?

What is the rhyme for porringer?
  The King he had a daughter fair,
And gave the Prince of Orange her.

Grey Goose and Gander

Grey goose and gander,
  Waft your wings together,
And carry the good king's daughter
  Over the one strand river.

Old King Cole

Old King Cole
  Was a merry old soul,
And a merry old soul was he;
  He called for his pipe,
  And he called for his bowl,
And he called for his fiddlers three.
Every fiddler had a fine fiddle,
  And a very fine fiddle had he;
Tweedle dee, tweedle dee, went the
    fiddlers three,
  Very merry men are we;
Oh there's none so rare
  As can compare
With King Cole and his fiddlers three.

Ten Little Men

Ten little men standing straight,
   Ten little men open the gate,
Ten little men all in a ring,
   Ten little men bow to the king,
Ten little men dance all day,
   Ten little men hide away.

When Famed King Arthur Ruled This Land

When famed King Arthur ruled this land
   He was a goodly king:
He took three pecks of barley meal
   To make a bag pudding.

A rare pudding the king did make,
   And stuffed it well with plums;
And in it put such lumps of fat,
   As big as my two thumbs.

The king and queen did eat thereof,
   And noblemen beside,
And what they could not eat that night
   The queen next morning fried.

There Was a King and he had Three Daughters

There was a king,
   And he had three daughters,
And they all lived,
   In a basin of water;
The basin bended,
   My story's ended.
If the basin had been stronger,
   My story would be longer.

The Queen of Hearts

The Queen of Hearts, she made some tarts,
   All on a summer's day;
The Knave of Hearts, he stole the tarts,
   And took them clean away.

The King of Hearts called for the tarts,
   And beat the Knave full sore;
The Knave of Hearts brought back the tarts,
   And vowed he'd steal no more.

Bunny Tails

Bunnies come in all different colours and sizes. Some have long ears and some have floppy ears. But all bunnies have fluffy tails. All except Alfie, that is. He had no tail at all and his friends teased him badly.

"Never mind, dear," said his mummy. "I love you, tail or no tail."

But Alfie did mind and at night he cried himself to sleep. Then one night he dreamt he met a fairy and told her all about his problem.

"A little fairy magic will soon fix that!" said the fairy. She took some dandelion clocks and sewed them together to make a lovely fluffy tail. "Turn around!" she said and fixed it in place in a flash.

Alfie woke with a start.

"If only my dream could come true," he thought sadly and looked down at his back. And there, to his astonishment, was a fine fluffy white tail!

"I'm a real bunny at last!" he said proudly, running off to show his new tail to his friends.

Tabby Cat and the Cockerel

Haven Farm is not only a hospital. There are also lots of animals who live on the farm all the time. One of these is Tabby the cat. She came to Haven Farm as a stray kitten, a long time ago. Sally and Joe fell in love with her straight away and Tabby soon became part of the family. Tabby likes nothing better than to curl up in a sunny, quiet corner of the barn. But there is one thing that spoils Tabby's peace and quiet – Charlie the cockerel.

"Poor Tabby," said Sally one day, as she stroked the cat's head. "She just doesn't like Charlie."

"Well, he is noisy and bossy," said Joe. Charlie was strutting along the gate, watching Tabby out of the corner of his eye.

"Cock-a-doodle-doo!" he crowed, loudly. Suddenly, Tabby jumped out of Sally's arms and ran towards the cockerel.

"No, Tabby, no!" shouted Sally. But, as Tabby leapt up at the cheeky cockerel, Charlie just fluttered into the safety of the hen house, clucking and squawking. This was a game that Tabby and Charlie had played many times before.

"Missed him again!" laughed Joe. Tabby just looked cross and walked off to the barn for some peace and quiet.

A few days later, Tabby wasn't really in the mood for Charlie's antics. Her ear was hurting and, every time Charlie crowed, it made her feel worse. So, she curled up in her favourite spot and tried to go to sleep. "Cock-a-doodle-doo!" cried Charlie, suddenly. Tabby screeched and fled across the farmyard. Charlie thought how clever he had been to scare Tabby and crowed loudly again.

"Hey, look at Tabby!" cried Joe. Sally looked up to see Tabby running across the yard, as fast as she could go. "Something's frightened her," said Joe.

Then they saw Charlie, looking very pleased with himself. They knew that he had been up to his old tricks again! "Come on, Joe," said Sally. "We must find Tabby." They walked towards the cow shed, where they had last seen her.

"Look!" said Joe. "There she goes." As they watched, Tabby ran straight up the side of the cow shed and jumped on to the roof.

"Oh, no!" said Sally. "We'll never get her now." At last, Tabby stopped running. That silly cockerel had really frightened her. Tabby looked around. The ground looked a long way down! She took a few, careful steps, but suddenly she felt very

dizzy and started to fall. Tabby landed with a bump! She had slipped off the roof and was now stuck between the cow shed and a wall!

"Miaooow!" she cried. Joe and Sally ran off to get Dad. They needed his help to rescue Tabby.

"Dad, come quick!" they shouted. "Tabby is in real trouble. She's just fallen off the roof!" Joe brought a cat carrier and Dad carried a special pole with a loop on the end of it.

Sally looked worried. "That won't hurt her, will it, Dad?" she asked.

"No, she just won't like it very much," said Dad, "but it's the safest way to catch her and pull her free." Dad squeezed his arm into the gap behind the cow shed. "I think I need to go on a diet," he joked. "You two had better make sure I don't get stuck as well!"

"Don't worry, Dad," said Joe. "We would rescue you." After a few tries, Dad slipped the loop over Tabby's head and gently pulled her towards him. She was crying and wriggling, as Dad put her into the cat basket.

"Right!" said Dad. "Let's take her to the surgery." Tabby sat on the examination table, while Dad gently checked her all over.

"Luckily, no bones broken," he said. Joe and Sally sighed with relief. Then, he used a special instrument to look in Tabby's ears. "But she has got a nasty ear infection," he said. "That would have made her dizzy. I'll give her some pills to make her better and we'll keep her indoors for a little while."

"No more Charlie-chasing for you," said Sally, giving Tabby a big cuddle later that day.

"Not yet, anyway," Tabby thought to herself. She settled down in a comfy armchair, pleased with all the fuss, and was soon fast asleep. She didn't see Charlie peeking in the window, to see if she was all right. Happy that Tabby was going to be fine, Charlie strutted back to the hen house and very quietly crowed... "Cock-a-doodle-doo!"

Being quiet wouldn't be too hard. Well, until Tabby was back to her good old self!

Fierce Tiger

Tiger wasn't really a tiger. He was a fierce stray kitten. People called him Tiger because he hissed and arched his back whenever they came near. "You really should be nicer to people," said his friend Tibbles. "They're not so bad once you train them."

But Tiger didn't trust people. If they came too near, he would show his claws and even give them a scratch. That soon taught them not to mess with Tiger. Tiger looked after himself. He didn't need anyone. At night he wandered the streets, searching dustbins for scraps and stealing food put out for pets. During the day, he slept wherever he could — under a bush, on top of a garage, and sometimes under the cars in an old scrapyard.

One cold winter's night, Tiger was wandering the streets when it began to snow. He spotted an open window.

"Aha," thought Tiger. "I bet it's warm and dry in there." He jumped through the window and found himself in a dark porch.

"This will do," thought Tiger. Tiger curled into a ball and was soon fast asleep. He was so comfortable that he slept all through the night. When he finally awoke, there was no one around. But beside him were a bowl of food and a dish of water.

"Don't mind if I do," purred Tiger. He gobbled down the whole lot, then drank some water before leaving through the window again. That day was colder than any Tiger had ever known so, when night fell and he saw the window open once more, he didn't hesitate to sneak in. This time, Tiger could see that the door from the porch was slightly ajar. He pushed it open and found himself in a warm kitchen. So he settled down and had a wonderful night's sleep. When he awoke in the morning, he found a bowl of delicious fish and a dish of water beside him.

"Don't mind if I do," purred Tiger. And he wolfed down the fish and lapped up the water before leaving. That night it was still snowing. Tiger returned once more. This time, when he went to settle himself beside the fire, he found a cosy basket there.

"Don't mind if I do," purred Tiger. And he crawled in and went to sleep. Tiger had never slept so well. In the morning, Tiger was woken by a rattling sound. Someone was in the kitchen. Tiger opened his left eye just a crack. A little boy was placing a bowl beside the basket. Tiger opened his eyes and stared at the little boy. The little boy stared at Tiger. Tiger leapt to his feet and got ready to hiss and scratch.

"Good boy," whispered the little boy, gently.

Tiger looked at the bowl. It was full of milk. "Don't mind if I do," he purred, and he drank the lot.

After that, Tiger returned to the house every night. Before long, he never slept anywhere else. The little boy always gave him plenty to eat and drink. And, in return, Tiger let the little boy stroke him and hold him on his lap.

One morning, Tiger was playing with the little boy in the garden, when his old friend Tibbles strolled past.

"I thought you didn't like people," meowed Tibbles.

"Oh," smiled Tiger, "they seem to be okay once you train them."

Tiger was no longer a fierce stray kitten!

The Invisible Imp

One day, Sarah Jones was pegging out her washing. It was a lovely day and she was looking forward to visiting her friend Rose. "I'll just get this washing on the line while the sun's shining," she said to herself, "and then I'll be on my way."

After a while, she stopped and looked down into the basket. "That's very peculiar!" she thought. "I know I've already pegged out that green shirt and there it is back in the basket." She carried on pegging out the clothes. Now she shook her head in disbelief. For, although she had been working away for quite a while, the basket of washing was still full and there was almost nothing on the line! She began to get quite cross, for she was going to be late getting to Rose's house.

Try as she might, she just could not get that washing pegged out. In the end, she had to leave the basket of wet washing and run to Rose's house.

"I'm so sorry I'm late, Rose," she gasped, all out of breath from running. Sarah told Rose all about what had happened.

"Well," said Rose, "that's a strange coincidence. I was baking some cakes for us to have for tea. Every time I put them in the oven and turned away, they were out of the oven and on the table again! In the end I had to stand guard over them – which reminds me, they were just beginning to cook nicely when you knocked on the door."

The two women went into Rose's kitchen and there were the cakes, sitting on the table again, half-cooked. "Now they're all ruined!" cried Rose. "Whatever shall we do?"

At that moment, there was a noise in the street. Rose and Sarah looked out of the window to see Elmer, the postman, surrounded by a crowd of people all shouting and waving envelopes in the air. The two women ran out into the street. "What's going on?" they cried.

"Elmer's given us all the wrong post," said Rose's neighbour, Dora. "He's normally so reliable, but this morning he seems to have gone completely crazy. Now we've got to sort out all the mail for him."

"I don't know what's happened," wailed Elmer in anguish. "I'm sure I posted all the letters through the right doors."

"Well," said Sarah, "Rose and I have found strange things happening to us this morning." She told the crowd their stories. Everyone forgave Elmer when they realised it wasn't his fault, but they were still truly mystified as to what – or who – could have caused all these problems.

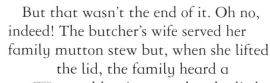

But that wasn't the end of it. Oh no, indeed! The butcher's wife served her family mutton stew but, when she lifted the lid, the family heard a bleating sound and a little lamb leaped out of the pot. The milkman delivered the milk as usual but, when people took their milk indoors, they found the bottles were full of lemonade. Old Mr Smith tried to pull his chair up to the table and found it was stuck hard to the floor. And, when Mrs Smith painted her bedroom blue, she came back and found it had changed to pink with purple spots.

Can you guess what had happened? Do you know who'd been up to all these tricks? It was an imp, of course! The wicked little fellow had become bored playing pranks on the fairies and goblins in fairyland. By now, they knew all his tricks and he was finding it harder and harder to catch them out. Then he had an idea. Why not play tricks in the human world where he would be invisible? So that's exactly what he did.

At first, he really only meant to play one or two tricks, but he had such fun that he couldn't resist carrying on.

Well, the invisible imp continued with his tricks. But of course, as you know, pride comes before a fall, and one day he just went too far. Sarah Jones had been invited to a party. It was to be a fancy dress party and on the invitation it said: *"Please wear red"*. Now Sarah fretted because she had no red clothes at all. Then she had an idea. She got out an old blue frock from the back of the cupboard. "I'll dye it red," she thought.

She mixed a big tub of red dye and was just about to put the dress into it, when along came the invisible imp. "Here's some fun!" he thought. "I'll turn the dye blue. Then she won't know why her dress hasn't changed colour. Won't that be funny!" And he started giggling to himself! He danced up and down on the edge of the tub, thinking up a really evil spell to turn the dye blue. But he laughed so much that he slipped and fell right into the bright red mixture. Fast as lightning out he scrambled and cast his spell.

Sure enough Sarah fished out the dress from the tub, and to her dismay saw that it was exactly the same colour as when she had put it into the dye. She was about to peer into the tub when something caught her eye. There, sitting on the table, chuckling and holding his sides with laughter, was a bright red imp. And there was a trail of tiny red footprints from the tub of dye to the table. The silly imp had no idea that he was no longer invisible and that he could be seen! In a flash Sarah realised what had happened. She chased the imp out of the house and down the street and, I'm glad to say, he wasn't able to play his mischievous tricks ever again.

Polly Piglet's Surprise Party

It was a lovely sunny day but
Polly Piglet was feeling sad. "It's my
birthday today," she said to herself. "But no one
seems to have remembered. Nobody has called to say happy birthday!"

Polly decided to go for a walk.
"Maybe my friends will remember if
they see me," she told herself and
went out into the farmyard.

"There's Holly Horse!"
thought Polly. Holly was inside
the stables looking very busy.
But, as soon as she saw Polly, she
stopped what she was doing and
began whistling.

"Hello Polly, nice day for a walk!" said Holly.

"Yes it is," said Polly. She waited a minute to see if
Holly was going to wish her happy birthday. But
Holly just went on whistling.

Just then, five little chicks came rushing past.
They looked as if they were on their way
somewhere very important. "Hello Polly, we
must rush, lots to do, have a nice walk!"

"Everyone's forgotten!" thought Polly crossly. "I was going to make a cake to share with my friends, but now I won't bother."

"There's Lolly Lamb," thought Polly. "She always remembers my birthday!" But, as soon as Lolly saw Polly, she ran off to the barn.

"What is going on?" wondered Polly. But then she saw that Lolly was beckoning Polly to follow her.

A tiny thought crept into Polly's mind, "Mmm, I wonder…?" And off she raced towards the barn, wagging her little curly tail. Dolly Cow was standing at the barn door.

"You've found us at last!" said Dolly smiling, and she stood back to let Polly step inside…

"Happy Birthday, Polly!" shouted Holly Horse, the five little chicks, Lolly Lamb, Dolly Cow and all of Polly's farmyard friends.

"Welcome to your surprise birthday party!"

Red Sky

Red sky at night,
   Shepherd's delight;
Red sky in the morning,
   Shepherd's warning.

Rain

Rain before seven,
   Fine by eleven.

Washing Up

When I was a little boy
   I washed my mummy's dishes;
I put my finger in one eye,
   And pulled out golden fishes.

What's the News?

What's the news of the day,
   Good neighbour, I pray?
They say the balloon
   Is gone up to the moon.

My Hobby Horse

I had a little hobby horse, it was well shod,
   It carried me to London, niddety nod,
And when we got to London we heard a great shout,
   Down fell my hobby horse and I cried out:
"Up again, hobby horse, if thou be a beast,
   When we get to our town we will have a feast,
And if there be but a little, why thou shall have some,
   And dance to the bag-pipes and beating of the drum."

Engine, Engine

Engine, engine, number nine,
Sliding down Chicago line;
When she's polished she will shine,
Engine, engine, number nine.

Robin Hood

Robin Hood
   Has gone to the wood;
He'll come back again
   If we are good.

Cobbler Cobbler

Cobbler, cobbler, mend my shoe,
  Get it done by half past two;
Stitch it up, and stitch it down,
  Then I'll give you half a crown.

And That's All

There was an old man,
  And he had a calf,
  And that's half;
He took him out of the stall,
  And put him on the wall,
  And that's all.

The Little Rusty, Dusty Miller

O the little rusty, dusty miller,
  Dusty was his coat,
    Dusty was his colour,
Dusty was the kiss
    I got from the miller.
If I had my pockets
  Full of gold and silver,
I would give it all
  To my dusty miller.

There Was a Little Boy

There was a little boy and a little girl
  Lived in an alley;
Says the little boy to the little girl,
  "Shall I, oh, shall I?"

Says the little girl to the little boy,
  "What shall we do?"
Says the little boy to the little girl,
  "I will kiss you."

Warning

The robin and the redbreast,
  The robin and the wren:
If you takes from their nest
  You'll never thrive again.

Mr East's Feast

Mr East gave a feast;
  Mr North laid the cloth;
Mr West did his best;
  Mr South burnt his mouth
With eating a cold potato.

Rumpelstiltskin

Once upon a time there was a boastful miller. One day, he told the king that his daughter was so clever that she could spin gold out of straw.

"I must meet this remarkable girl," said the king. "Bring her to the palace at once."

The king took the miller's daughter to a room filled with straw. In one corner stood a spinning wheel. "You must spin all this straw into gold before morning," the king told the girl, "or you will be put to death." Then he went out and locked the door behind him.

The poor girl sat at the spinning wheel and wept. However could she make gold from straw? Suddenly, the door flew open, and in leapt a funny-looking little man.

"Why are you crying?" he asked.

When the girl told him what the king had said, the strange man replied, "What will you give me if I spin this straw into gold for you?"

"My pearl necklace," said the girl.

So the little man sat down at the spinning wheel and quickly spun all the straw into gold. Then he magically vanished from the room.

The next morning, the king was amazed at all the gold – but now he wanted even more. He took the girl to a bigger room, and had it filled with straw. Once again, he told her to spin the straw into gold by morning, or she would die. Then he left.

The poor girl sat down and wept. Suddenly, the odd little man appeared. "What will you give me if I help you this time?" he asked.

"My pretty ring," the girl replied.

So the little man began to spin, and soon all the straw had been turned into gold. Then he vanished.

The next morning the greedy king was astounded but still not satisfied. He took the girl to an even bigger room, piled to the ceiling with straw. "If you succeed this time, you will become queen," the king said. "If you

fail, you know what will happen."

As soon as the girl was alone, the little man appeared. "I have nothing left to give you," said the girl.

"Then promise me your first-born child when you become queen," said the man.

"I might never become queen and I may never have a child," the girl thought, and so she promised.

So the strange little man sat down at the spinning wheel and began to work. He spun for many hours and the pile of gold grew higher and higher.

"At last," said the little man, "my task is done." Then he vanished. The girl gazed around the room. It was stacked from floor to ceiling with glistening gold that shone like the sun.

At dawn, the king was overjoyed. He kept his promise and soon married the miller's daughter.

The whole kingdom rejoiced, and the king and his new queen were very happy together.

A year later, the king and queen had a baby. By this time, the queen had forgotten all about her promise – but the funny little man had not. One night, he appeared in the queen's bedchamber. "I have come for your baby!" he announced gleefully.

"No!" cried the queen. "I will give you jewels, gold, anything you wish! But please do not take my baby." She wept so miserably that the little man took pity on her.

"Very well," he said. "If you can guess my name within three nights you may keep your baby. If not, the child is mine!" Then he disappeared.

The queen sent messengers out to gather names from every town and village in the kingdom. They returned with thousands of suggestions. Over the next two evenings, when the little man arrived, the queen questioned him again and again:

"Is your name Tom?"

"No," replied the strange little man.

"Jack? Dick? Peter?" she asked. The strange man shook his head. "Could it be Brutus or Clarence, then?"

Each time, the reply was the same: "No, Your Majesty."

By the third day, only one messenger had not returned. Late that afternoon, he was on his way back to the palace when he saw a hut in a forest clearing. In front of it, an odd little man was dancing around a fire, singing:

"I'll be the winner of this game!
The queen will never guess my name!
She will lose, and I will win,
Because my name is...
Rumpelstiltskin!"

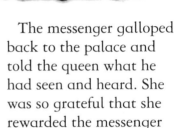

The messenger galloped back to the palace and told the queen what he had seen and heard. She was so grateful that she rewarded the messenger with a huge sack of gold.

That night, the queen eagerly waited in her throne room for the little man. When he appeared, the queen asked, "Is your name Guzzletum?"

"No, it's not!" laughed the little man.

"Is it Bumblebottom? Jigglejoggle? Tickletooth or Wigglewoggle?"

"No! No!" he cackled. "Your time's running out, Your Majesty!"

The queen smiled. "Could it be... Rumpelstiltskin?"

The little man could not believe his ears and flew into a rage. "Who told you? Who told you?" he shrieked. "How did you find out?"

He cried and squealed and beat the floor with his fists.

"You've won! You've won!" he wailed, and disappeared in a shower of sparks.

The little man never came back to worry the queen again, and they all lived happily ever after.

Little Bunny and the Bully

Down in Cowslip Meadow lived lots and lots of bunnies. They were all friends and played together happily all day long – all except for one. Big Bunny was a bully! He didn't like the other bunnies having fun and was always teasing and scaring them! He'd hide behind bushes and jump out on them and pull the girls' ears and tweak their tails!

Big Bunny didn't have any friends or anyone to play with, because he was always so mean. But he didn't care!

"Who needs friends, anyway?" he said. "Not me!" And off he hopped, down to the stream. But one of the bunnies felt sorry for Big Bunny.

"Everyone should have a friend," thought Little Bunny, as he hopped after the rabbit. "Hey, Big Bunny," he called. "Would you like to share my carrot cake and be my friend?"

"No!" snarled the naughty bully. "I don't want to share. I want it all!"

And with one, big bunny bounce, he grabbed the yummy cake and knocked Little Bunny into the water – SPLOOSH! "I don't like sharing!" cried Big Bunny, hopping away. "And I don't want you to be my friend!"

Little Bunny shook himself dry and hopped back towards the meadow. "I'm going home," he muttered to himself. "Big Bunny is such a bully."

Suddenly, he heard a noise. It sounded like someone crying. "I wonder what that is?" thought Little Bunny. Following the noise, he hopped towards the edge of a steep bank and peeped over. There, at the very bottom, sat Big Bunny!

"Please help me, Little Bunny!" he called, weakly. "I've hurt my paw and I can't climb up!" Little Bunny bounced into action!

"Don't worry, I'll get some help!" he called to Big Bunny and raced off home, as fast as he could.

And even though Big Bunny had always been so mean to the other rabbits of Cowslip Meadow, when Little Bunny cried, "Big Bunny is hurt," they all rushed to help.

Little Bunny's daddy climbed down the bank and rescued the scared, injured rabbit.

"I'm sorry for being so nasty to you," cried Big Bunny, as he gave Little Bunny a big hug. "Thank you for saving me!"

"Well, that's what friends are for!" chuckled Little Bunny and everyone cheered!

Leap Frog

"Whee! Look at me! Look at me!" yelled Springy, the frog, as he went leaping through the air, jumping from one lily pad to the other with a great splash. "I'm the bounciest frog in the whole wide world! Whee!"

"Tut, tut!" quacked Mother Duck. "That young frog is a nuisance. He never looks where he's going, and he doesn't mind who he splashes."

"Quite dreadful," agreed Downy, the swan. "And he makes so much noise. Sometimes it's hard to hear yourself think!"

But Springy wasn't listening. He was far too busy jumping across the lily pads as high as he could.

"Come on!" he called to the little ducklings. "Come over here, we'll have a diving contest!"

"He's a bad influence on our youngsters," Mother Duck went on. "If only something could be done about him."

"I suppose it's just high spirits," said Downy. "He'll grow out of it."

But Springy didn't grow out of it – he grew worse. He would wake everyone up at the crack of dawn, singing loudly at the top of his croaky voice.

"Here comes the day, it's time to play, hip hooray, hip hooray!" And he would leap from place to place, waking up the ducks and swans in their nests, calling down Rabbit's burrow, and shouting into Water Rat's hole in the bank. Of course, Springy just thought that he was being friendly. He didn't realise that everyone was getting fed up with him.

"I'm all for a bit of fun," said Water Rat. "But young Springy always takes things too far."

Then, one day, Springy appeared
almost bursting with excitement.

"Listen everyone," he called. "There's
going to be a jumping competition on the
other side of the pond. All the other frogs from
miles around are coming. But I'm sure to win,
because I'm the bounciest frog in the whole wide world!"

The day of the contest dawned, and everyone gathered at the far side
of the pond to watch the competition. Springy had never seen so many
frogs in one place before. But, to Springy's amazement, *all* the frogs
could jump high, and far. They sprang gracefully across the lily pads,
cheered on by the crowd.

Springy was going to have to jump higher and further than ever if he
wanted to win. At last it was his turn. "Good luck!" cried the ducklings.

Springy took his place on the starting pad, then, gathering all his
strength, he leapt up high and flew through the air, further and further,
past the finish line, and on, until – GULP! He landed right in crafty
Pike's waiting open mouth! As usual, Springy had not been looking
where he was going!

The naughty pike swallowed Springy in one gulp, then dived down

and hid in the middle of the pond. Everyone looked around in dismay – Springy was gone.

Well, there was no doubt about it. Springy had jumped the highest, and the furthest.

"I declare Springy the winner," Warty, the toad, who had organised the contest, said glumly.

After that, things were much quieter for the other folk who lived around the pond. But, instead of enjoying the peace, they found that they rather missed Springy.

"He was a cheery little frog," said Downy.

But, deep in the pond, Pike was feeling sorry for himself. He thought he'd been very clever catching that frog, but he'd had terrible indigestion ever since. You see, Springy was still busy jumping away inside him! Pike rose up to the top of the water, and gulped at the air. And, as he did so, out jumped Springy!

Everyone was delighted to see him, and cheered as they gave him the medal for winning the jumping contest.

"This is wonderful," said Springy. "But I have learned my lesson – from now on I'll look before I leap!" and he hopped away quietly to play with the ducklings.

Sparky the Baby Dragon

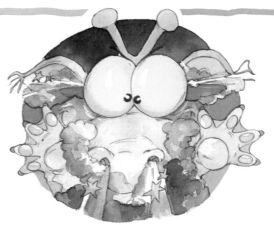

Sparky was a young dragon who lived in a cave far, far away. Now, as you know, dragons can breathe flames out of their noses! But you may not know that baby dragons have to learn how to do it. "Watch me," said Mum to Sparky. She puffed out a long flame and lit a candle.

"Now watch me," said Dad, and he breathed over some logs in the fireplace and made a fire. Sparky watched very carefully.

"Now watch me," he said, and he puffed until he was purple in the face. Two or three little sparks came out of his nose and ears!

"Bravo!" said Dad. "It's coming on!" said Mum. Sparky felt very proud.

One day Mum and Dad had to go out. "Stay indoors," they told Sparky. "Don't go out, and don't let anybody in. The wicked witch hates little dragons and turns them into teapots, just for fun!"

"Oh!" said Sparky. But he didn't mind staying in. He had some new toy knight figures to play with. He had just started when he heard a bell outside. "Ting-a-ling," it went, "ting-a-ling." And then a voice said, "Ice cream! Ice cream! Come and get your ice cream!"

Sparky peeped out. Outside was a brightly painted ice cream cart and sitting behind the wheel was an old woman with a big grin. Then the woman laughed! It was a loud, cackling laugh and when Sparky heard it, he knew it was the witch. He slammed the door and locked it.

"Phew!" thought Sparky. "That was close." The afternoon passed peacefully. Then, the doorbell rang. "Who is it?" Sparky called out.

"It's Uncle Jack," said a voice, "I've come to take you fishing." Sparky liked Uncle Jack, and he liked fishing!

"Is it really you?" he asked. "Of course it is," laughed Uncle Jack. But, as soon as Sparky heard the loud, cackling laugh, he knew it was the witch.

"Go away!" he shouted. Then he heard someone crying. He peered through the door and saw a baby dragon on the doorstep!

"I've lost my mummy!" sobbed the dragon. "You'd better come in," said Sparky. He opened the door and the baby dragon rushed in. Then…

"Got you!" snapped the baby dragon – and turned into the witch! Sparky gasped. The witch raised her wand and shouted the magic words "Ta-ra-ra-boom-de-ay" and started to spin very fast.

Sparky puffed as hard as he could. Then he had a big surprise! The witch was surrounded by a puff of smoke. Then, as the smoke cleared, he saw that she had turned into a teapot!

Just then Mum and Dad came back. "Have you had any trouble while we've been away?" asked Mum, kissing him.

"Not much!" said Sparky. "But, next time you go out, can I come with you?"

"Of course you can!" said Mum. "Now why don't I make some tea in this nice new teapot!"

Catch Him

Catch him, crow! Carry him, kite!
  Take him away till the apples are ripe;
When they are ripe and ready to fall,
  Here comes a baby, apples and all.

Jack-a-Dandy

Nauty pauty Jack-a-Dandy
  Stole a piece of sugar candy
From the grocer's shoppy shop,
  And away did hoppy-hop.

Wine and Cakes

Wine and cakes for gentlemen,
  Hay and corn for horses,
A cup of ale for good old wives,
  And kisses for the lasses.

Punctuate

Every lady in this land
  Has twenty nails upon each hand.
Five and twenty on hands and feet
  All this is true without deceit.

Marching

March, march, head erect,
  Left, right, that's correct.

Did You See My Wife?

Did you see my wife, did you see, did you see,
  Did you see my wife looking for me?
She wears a straw bonnet, with white ribbands on it,
  And diminity petticoats over her knee.

Rain

Rain, rain,
  go to Spain,
Never show
  your face again.

Tommy's Shop

Tommy kept a chandler's shop,
  Richard went to buy a mop;
Tommy gave him such a whop,
  That sent him out of the chandler's shop.

King Boggen

King Boggen, he built a fine new hall;
Pastry and piecrust, that was the wall;
The windows were made of black pudding and white,
Roofed with pancakes – you never saw the like.

Pit, Pat

Pit, pat, well-a-day,
   Little Robin flew away;
Where can little robin be?
   Gone into the cherry tree.

Bagpipes

Puss came dancing out of
   a barn
   With a pair of bagpipes
     under her arm;
She could sing nothing but,
    Fiddle cum fee,
   The mouse has married the humble-bee.
Pipe, cat – dance, mouse –
   We'll have a wedding at our good house.

Green Cheese

   Green cheese,
   Yellow laces,
   Up and down
   The market places.

The Priest

The little priest of Felton,
The little priest of Felton,
He killed a mouse within his house,
And nobody there to help him.

Shrovetide

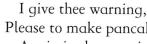
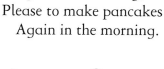

Once, twice, thrice,
   I give thee warning,
Please to make pancakes
   Again in the morning.

Mother?

"Mother, may I go out to swim?"
   "Yes, my darling daughter.
Fold your clothes up neat and trim,
   But don't go near the water."

The Lost Lion

Once there was a lion cub called Lenny. He was a very tiny lion cub, but he was sure that he was the bravest lion in the whole of Africa. When his mother taught her cubs how to stalk prey, Lenny would stalk his mother and pounce on her. When she showed them how to wash their faces, Lenny licked his sister's face so that she growled at him. When the mother lioness led her cubs down to the watering hole to drink, he jumped into the water and created a huge splash that soaked everyone.

The other lionesses were not amused. "You'd better watch that son of yours," they said to Lenny's mother, "or he'll get into really big trouble."

One day the mother lioness led her cubs on their first big hunt. "Stay close to me," she said, "or you could get hurt."

She crawled off through the undergrowth with her cubs following on behind, one after the other. Lenny was at the back. The grass tickled his tummy and he wanted to laugh, but he was trying hard to be obedient. So he crawled along, making sure he kept the bobbing tail of the cub in front in his sight.

On and on they crawled until Lenny was beginning to feel quite weary. "But a brave lion cub doesn't give up," he thought to himself. And on he plodded.

At last the grass gave way to a clearing. Lenny looked up, and to his dismay he saw that the tail he had been following was attached, not to one of his brothers or sisters, but to a baby elephant!

Somewhere along the trail he had started following the wrong tail and now he was hopelessly lost. He wanted to cry out for his mother but then he remembered that he was the bravest lion in all of Africa. So what do you think he did? He went straight up to the mother elephant and growled his fiercest growl at her. "That'll frighten her!" thought Lenny. "She won't dare growl back!" And, of course, she didn't growl back. Instead she lifted her trunk and trumpeted so loudly at Lenny that he was blown off his feet and through the air and landed against the hard trunk of a tree.

Lenny got up and found that his knees were knocking.

"Oh my," he thought, "that elephant has a very loud growl. But I'm still definitely the bravest lion in all of Africa." He set off across the plain. It was getting hot in the midday sun and soon Lenny began to feel sleepy. "I'll just take a nap in that tree," he thought, and started climbing up into the branches.

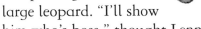

To his surprise, he found that the tree was already occupied by a large leopard. "I'll show him who's boss," thought Lenny, baring his tiny claws. The leopard raised his head to look at Lenny, and then bared his own huge, razor-sharp claws. He took a swipe at Lenny with his paw. Without even touching Lenny, the wind from the leopard's great paw swept Lenny out of the tree and he landed with a bump on the ground.

When Lenny got up he found that his legs were trembling. "Oh my," he thought, "that leopard had big claws. But I'm still definitely the bravest lion in Africa." He set off again across the plain. After a while he began to feel quite hungry. "I wonder what I can find to eat," he thought. Just then he saw a spotted shape lying low in the grass. "That looks like a tasty meal," thought Lenny as he pounced on the spotted shape. But the spotted shape was a cheetah! Quick as a flash, the cheetah sprang away and, as he did so, his tail caught Lenny a blow that sent him spinning round and round in circles.

When Lenny stopped spinning, he got up and found his whole body was shaking. "Oh my," he thought, "that cheetah is a fast runner." Then he added in rather a small voice, "But I'm still the bravest lion in Africa."

He set off again across the plain. By now it was getting dark and Lenny was wishing he was at home with his mother and brothers and sisters. "I wonder if they've noticed I've gone," he thought sadly as a tear rolled down his furry cheek. He felt cold and tired and hungry as he crawled into the undergrowth to sleep.

Some time later Lenny was woken by a noise that was louder than anything he'd ever heard before – louder even than the elephant's trumpeting. It filled the night air and made the leaves on the trees shake. The noise was getting louder and louder and the animal that was making it was getting nearer and nearer. Lenny peeped out from his hiding place and saw a huge golden creature with big yellow eyes that shone in the dark like lamps. It had a great crown of shaggy golden fur all around its head and its red jaws were open wide revealing a set of very large white fangs. How it roared! Lenny was terrified and about to turn tail and run, when the animal stopped roaring and spoke to him. "Come here, Lenny," said the animal gently. "It's me, your father, and I'm going to take you home. Climb up on my back, little one."

So Lenny climbed up on his father's back and was carried all the way home. And when they got there his father told his mother and his brothers and sisters that Lenny had been a very brave lion after all.

Peter, Peter, Pumpkin Eater

Peter, Peter, pumpkin eater,
   Had a wife and couldn't keep her;
He put her in a pumpkin shell
   And there he kept her very well.

Peter, Peter, pumpkin eater,
   Had another and didn't love her;
Peter learned to read and spell,
   And then he loved her very well.

Simple Simon

Simple Simon met a pieman
   Going to the fair;
Said Simple Simon to the pieman,
   "Let me taste your ware."

Said the pieman to Simple Simon,
   "Show me first your penny";
Said Simple Simon to the pieman,
   "Indeed I have not any."

There Was a Little Boy

There was a little boy went into a barn,
   And lay down on some hay;
An owl came out and flew about,
   And the little boy ran away.

Johnny Shall Have a New Bonnet

Johnny shall have a new bonnet,
   And Johnny shall go to the fair,
And Johnny shall have a blue ribbon
   To tie up his bonny brown hair.

Wee Willie Winkie

Wee Willie Winkie runs through the town,
  Upstairs and downstairs in his nightgown,
Peeping through the keyhole, crying through the lock,
  "Are the children in their beds, it's past eight o'clock?"

Billy Booster

Billy Billy Booster,
  Had a little rooster,
The rooster died
  And Billy cried.
Poor Billy Booster.

Tommy Snooks and Bessy Brooks

As Tommy Snooks and Bessy Brooks
  Were walking out one Sunday,
Says Tommy Snooks to Bessy Brooks,
  "Tomorrow will be Monday."

When Jacky's a Very Good Boy

When Jacky's a very good boy,
  He shall have cakes and a custard;
But when he does nothing but cry,
  He shall have nothing but mustard.

Little Tommy Tucker

Little Tommy Tucker
  Sings for his supper:
What shall we give him?
  Brown bread and butter.
How shall he cut it
  Without a knife?
How can he marry
  Without a wife?

Little Bunny

Come, Little Bunny,
   say "Good night".
There's lots to do
   before you turn out the light.

Collect all your toys and
   put them away.
Kiss them good night –
   it's the end of the day.

Hop in the bath for a
   rinse and a scrub.
Play with the bubbles –
   rub-a-dub-dub-dub!

Finish your story and turn
   out the light.
Time to tuck you in warmly
   and kiss you goodnight.

Good night!

Sweet dreams, Little Bunny,
   we love you.
And Mr Moon says
   "Good night" too.

Little Bear

Look through the window at the
   moon shining bright.
Who can you see in the twinkling
   starlight?

Up in the trees,
   the grey doves coo.
Calling a friendly
   "Good night" to you.

Good night, little squirrel.
   Good night, little mouse.
Hurrying, scurrying to bed
   in the house.

Close your eyes, Little Bear,
   and turn out the light.
Fall asleep like your friends,
   with eyes closed tight.

Listen to Owl calling
   "Who-whoo-whooo!"
While old Mr Moon
   watches over you.

Good night!

The Squeaky Van

Honk! Honk! went the horn on the old blue van. It was market day, and Dad was getting impatient. "Hurry up, you two," he called. "I want to get to the market early."

Dad reversed the old blue van out of the shed, and Rosie and Danny piled into the front. They all waved goodbye to Mum. Conker chased the van out of the farmyard barking loudly. Honk! Honk! Dad hooted at Joe as they passed him on the tractor.

"This van must be a hundred years old," muttered Danny, as they jolted over the bumpy road. "When are we going to get a new one?"

"I don't want a new one," protested Rosie. "Mum says this van has been at home since I was a baby."

"No, it's been at Faraway Farm since Grandad was a baby," laughed Dad. "And it still runs perfectly." But, as they were going down a long hill, Dad looked puzzled.

"Can you hear a funny sort of squeaking?" he asked.

THE SQUEAKY VAN

"I think I can hear something," said Rosie. "But it's not very loud."
Dad stopped in a lay-by and got out. He lifted the bonnet
and poked around in
the engine.

"I can't hear anything
now," he said, scratching
his head. "But we'll call
in to Tom's garage.
Perhaps he can see if
anything is wrong."

Soon they arrived at
Tom's garage. "Morning,
Tom," said Dad. "We've
got a little problem
with the van."

"We've got a squeak,"
added Rosie.

"I'll take a look," Tom gave her a big wink. "Maybe there's a mouse in
the engine!" Tom peered at the engine. He checked the oil, fiddled with
the fan belt, and poured water into the radiator.
Then he started the engine again.

"I can't hear anything wrong," he announced.
"The van's old but it should go on for a
while yet."

They thanked Tom and drove into town.
Everywhere was crowded because it was market
day. Dad parked the van and they all got out.
"Ooh, look!" Rosie pointed excitedly. "There's a
roundabout. Can we have a ride?"

"Maybe later," replied Dad. "I must buy some tools and other bits and pieces first."

"And I want to go to the pet stall and buy a new collar for Conker," added Danny.

When they had bought everything they needed, Rosie had two rides on the roundabout. "That was great," she smiled.

"Now, let's get an ice cream," said Danny. Dad bought ice creams and loaded the van while Danny and Rosie ate them. Then they all jumped into the van and set off for home. "There's that squeak again," said Rosie. "It's getting louder."

"I'll ask Joe to look underneath when we get home," said Dad, frowning.

"I don't think it's coming from the engine," said Danny.

"No, it's coming from the back," cried Rosie.

Before long they turned into the yard of Faraway Farm. Dad stopped the engine and they all went round to the back to unload.

THE SQUEAKY VAN

"Shhh!" whispered Danny. "I can hear something."

He lifted up the floor of the van. There, sitting in the middle of the spare tyre was a fat brown hen with four tiny yellow chicks chirping at the tops of their voices. "Well, would you believe it?" said Dad, laughing. "That crafty old hen must have got inside and made a nest when the van was parked in the barn."

"Let me see," said Rosie, pushing between them.

"That explains it," smiled Dad. "To start with there was just one chick chirping and then as the others hatched out, the squeaking got louder."

"What about the nest?" asked Danny. "There are still three eggs left."

"We'll just leave them," smiled Dad. "I don't mind the hen using the tyre for a nest."

Just then Mum came out. "We've brought you back a surprise from market," laughed Danny.

"Some new babies!" said Rosie.

A Goodnight Kiss

"It's bedtime now, Oakey," said Mum. Oakey curled up in the chair. His ears began to droop and he muttered, "Oh, that's not fair!"

"Have a drink first," smiled Mum, "then you must go."

"Five minutes more!" begged Oakey.

Mum answered, "No!"

Oakey's ears drooped and off he went. But he was back in a flash! "Where's your drink?" asked Mum. "You haven't been very long. You look scared, Oakey. Is there something wrong?"

"There's a monster in the kitchen, with long, white shaggy hair, lurking in the corner, behind the rocking chair," said Oakey.

Mum laughed. "Oh, Oakey, you've made a mistake. That's no monster. It's a mop." And she gave the mop a shake.

Oakey's ears drooped and off he went. But he was back in a flash! "What's the matter?" asked Mum.

"There's a ghost in the hallway, hovering around. Look, there it is floating just above the ground," he wailed.

"Oh, Oakey, you've made a mistake. That's no ghost. It's just an old coat, hanging on the hook. Coats don't float!" laughed Mum.

A Goodnight Kiss

Oakey's ears drooped and off he went. But he was back in a flash! "Why aren't you in bed, Oakey?" asked Mum.

"There's a great big lump beneath the sheets. It's waiting to get me. I'm scared it's going to pounce. Please come and see," sniffed Oakey.

"Oh, Oakey, you've made a mistake. The only thing underneath the sheets is your old teddy bear," smiled Mum.

Oakey's ears drooped and he got into bed. But he didn't close his eyes. "Why aren't you asleep?" asked Mum.

"There are huge creepy crawlies underneath my bed. And I can't get the thought of them out of my head," complained Oakey.

"They're just your slippers, Oakey, so there's no need to hide. They won't be creeping anywhere without your feet inside," grinned Mum. "That's it now, Oakey. Time to say goodnight."

Mum left the room, switching off the light. And then Oakey saw it by the door. The monster! It moved across the floor and walked straight towards him, with its arms stretched out. Oakey's mouth opened, but he found he couldn't shout. The monster leaned over him and Oakey closed his eyes. What happened next gave Oakey an enormous surprise. The monster picked him up and cuddled him tight. Monsters just don't do that.

This couldn't be right! Then Mum's voice whispered, "Don't worry, it's just me. When I said 'Goodnight' just now, I forgot to give you this." Then Monster Mum gave Oakey a goodnight kiss!

Night Sounds

Midnight's bell goes ting, ting, ting, ting, ting,
   Then dogs do howl, and not a bird does sing
But the nightingale, and she cries twit, twit, twit;
   Owls then on every bough do sit;
Ravens croak on chimneys' tops;
   The cricket in the chamber hops;
The nibbling mouse is not asleep,
   But he goes peep, peep,
     peep, peep, peep;
And the cats cry mew,
   mew, mew,
And still the cats cry mew,
   mew, mew.

In Dreams

Beyond, beyond the mountain line,
   The greystone and the boulder,
Beyond the growth of dark green pine,
   That crowns its western shoulder,
There lies that fairy land of mine,
   Unseen of a beholder.
Ah me! they say if I could stand
   Upon those mountain ledges,
I should but see on either hand
   Plain fields and dusty hedges:
And yet I know my fairy land
   Lies somewhere o'er their hedges.

My Shadow

I have a little shadow that goes in and out with me,
   And what can be the use of him is more than I can see.
He is very, very like me from the heels up to the head;
   And I see him jump before me, when I jump into my bed.

One morning, very early, before the sun was up,
   I rose and found the shining dew on every buttercup;
But my lazy little shadow, like an arrant sleepyhead,
   Had stayed at home behind me and was fast asleep in bed.

From a Railway Carriage

Faster than fairies, faster than witches,
  Bridges and houses, hedges and ditches;
And charging along like troops in a battle,
  All through the meadows the horses and cattle:
All of the sights of the hill and the plain
  Fly as thick as driving rain;
And ever again, in the wink of an eye,
  Painted stations whistle by.

Here is a child who clambers and scrambles,
  All by himself and gathering brambles;
Here is a tramp who stands and gazes;
  And there is the green for stringing the daisies!
Here is a cart run away in the road
  Lumping along with man and load;
And here is a mill, and there is a river:
  Each a glimpse and gone for ever!

Good Night

Good night, God bless you,
  Go to bed and undress you.

Good night, sweet repose,
  Half the bed and all the clothes.

The Wind

Who has seen the wind?
  Neither I nor you;
But when the leaves
  hang trembling
The wind is
  passing through.

Who has seen the wind?
  Neither you nor I;
But when the trees bow
  down their heads
The wind is passing by.

Spellbound

The night is darkening round me,
  The wild winds coldly blow;
But a tyrant spell has bound me
  And I cannot, cannot go.
The giant trees are bending
  Their bare boughs weighed
    with snow.
And the storm is fast descending,
  And yet I cannot go.

Clouds beyond clouds above me,
  Wastes beyond wastes below;
    But nothing drear can
      move me;
  I will not, cannot go.

Night-night Bear

Teddy Bear had been to the circus. "It's very late – why don't you have a nap in the back of the car," said Mummy Bear kindly.

"I'm not sleepy!" said Teddy Bear, stifling a yawn. "Weren't the clowns funny? I loved the clowns best."

"The trapeze artists were amazing," said Mummy Bear.

"Oh, they were the best of all," agreed Teddy Bear. "When I grow up I'm going to fly on the trapeze."

"I thought you were going to be a clown," said Daddy Bear, smiling.

"I'll be a clown in my spare time," yawned Teddy Bear.

"What about the trick riders?" asked a smiling Mummy Bear.

"I'll do that as well," sighed Teddy Bear, resting his head against a cushion.

All the way home Teddy Bear dreamed about working in the circus. In his dream he could do everything – he made people laugh and cry and gasp in amazement.

"Night-night Circus Bear," said Daddy Bear, carrying him upstairs to his bed.

"Night-night Daddy," mumbled Teddy Bear through his dreams.

Index

Adam and Eve and
Pinchme 301
All at Sea 100
All the Bells Were
Ringing 252
Alone 252
And That's All 349
As I Walked by
Myself 92
As I Was Going
Along 45
Back to the Farm 237
Bagpipes 365
Barney the Boastful
Bear 254
Bear Finds a Friend 318
Bear's Picnic 319
Benny the Barmy
Builder 102
Betty Pringle 92
Billy Booster 371
Birthday Bear 246
Birthday Bunnies 62
Bless You 37
Blow, Wind, Blow! 29
Bob Robin 189
Bobby's Best Birthday
Present 52
Bone Crazy 186
Bottoms Up! 278
Bouncy Bunny 224
Bow-wow 36
Boy Who Wished Too
Much, The 326
Bread and Milk for
Breakfast 253
Bumble Bee Helps
Out 238
Bunny Olympics,
The 20
Bunny Tails 334
Buried Treasure 144
Busy Farmer 236
Catch Him 364
Chalk and Cheese 250
Charlie Wag 317
Charlie Warley 11
Chasing Tails 314
Cheeky Chick 324

Chicklings, The 132
Chirpy Chatty
Chicks, The 39
Clap Hands 220
Clap Your Hands 29
Clap, Clap Hands 141
Clip, Clop! 285
Clumsy Fred 270
Cobbler, Cobbler 349
Cock-a-Doodle-Doo 173
Counting Sheep 284
Crocodile Smiles 158
Cuckoo, The 157
Cushy Cow Bonny 77
Custard's New Home 74
Daddy 11
Daffy-Down-Dilly 76
Dame Trot 316
Dance, Thumbkin,
Dance 220
Danny Duckling in
Trouble 170
Desmond Grows
Up 164
Did You Know? 236
Did You See My
Wife? 364
Diddlety, Diddlety 37
Dingle Dangle
Scarecrow 19
Don't Care 178
Dotty Professor, The 222
Ducks for a Day 78
Duel, The 179
Easter Bunnies 266
Ebby, the Smallest
Pup 330
Eeper, Weeper 316
Egg Hatching
Dream 285
Eldorado 179
Engine, Engine 348
Face Game, A 220
Fierce Tiger 340
Fire on the
Mountain 93
Five Fat Sausages 205
Five Little Monkeys 60
Five Little Peas 205

Five Little Soldiers 141
Fluff Monsters, The 154
Follow My Bangalorey
Man 44
Foxy's Hole 140
Fred the Fearless
Fireman 118
From a Railway
Carriage 381
From Wibbleton
to Wobbleton 45
Giant, The 10
Girls and Boys Come
Out to Play 173
Go to Bed 316
Go to Bed, Tom 11
Going Downhill on
a Bicycle 253
Golden Bird, The 150
Goodnight 381
Goodnight Kiss,
A 378
Good Old Days,
The 40
Good Teamwork 230
Goosey Goosey
Gander 172
Grand Old Duke of
York, The 332
Great Egg Hunt,
The 31
Greedy Bear 128
Greedy Tom 37
Green Cheese 365
Grey Goose and
Gander 332
Handy Spandy, Jack-a-
Dandy 124
Hannah Bantry 316
Hark the Robbers, 124
Harry Parry 188
Haunted House,
The 139
Head, Shoulders,
Knees and Toes 140
Hector Protector 77
Here's the Lady's Knives
and Forks 221
Hey, Diddle, Diddle 19

Hey, Dorolot,
Dorolot! 300
Hide and Seek 116
Higgledy Piggledy 109
Higglety, Pigglety,
Pop! 77
Hippo's Holiday 134
Home Sweet Home 282
Honey Bear and the
Bees 286
Hooray for Pepper 142
Horse of Course!, A 285
Horse Power 22
Hot Cross Buns! 204
Humpty Dumpty 76
Hurt No Living Thing
253
I Can… 109
I Do Not Like Thee 317
I Hear Thunder 125
I Love Sixpence 61
I Saw a Slippery,
Slithery Snake 140
I Wish… 180
If a Pig Wore a Wig 189
If All the World was
Apple-pie 93
If Wishes Were
Horses 92
If You Hold My Hand
148
If You're Happy and
You Know It 19
In Dreams 380
Intery, Mintery,
Cutery, Corn 156
Invisible Imp, The 342
It's Not Fair 127
It's Raining, It's
Pouring 28
Jack and Guy 189
Jack and Jill 173
Jack and the
Beanstalk 110
Jack be Nimble 92
Jack Sprat 269
Jack, Jack, the Bread's
a-Burning 188
Jack-a-Dandy 364

Jackanory 29
Jay-bird 157
Jim Crow 108
John Smith 10
Johnny Shall Have
a New Bonnet 370
King Boggen 365
Kittens are Cuddly 237
Knick Knack Paddy
Whack 172
Lazy Teddy 96
Leap Frog 358
Leg Over Leg 140
Leo Makes a Friend 46
Lie a-Bed 109
Little Bear 373
Little Blue Ben 316
Little Bunny 372
Little Bunny and
the Bully 356
Little Chick Lost 260
Little Dog Lost 206
Little Hare 10
Little Jack Jingle 188
Little Robin Redbreast
156
Little Rusty, Dusty
Miller, The 349
Little Tim and his
Brother Sam 174
Little Tommy
Tittlemouse 188
Little Tommy Tucker
371
Little Wind 157
Littlest Pig, The 86
Lizzie and the Tractor 84
Lost and Alone 26
Lost for Ever 182
Lost Lion, The 366
Loves to Sing! 236
Magic Tree, The 48
Magpies 157
Making a Splash! 90
Man in the Wilderness,
The 93
Marching 364
Me, Myself, and I 300
Mean King and the

Crafty Lad, The 294
Michael Finnegan 268
Milking 37
Milly the Greedy
 Puppy 190
Monkey Mayhem 80
Monty the
 Mongrel 234
Moo! Moo! Moo! 284
Mother? 365
Mouse's Lullaby, The 179
Mr East's Feast 349
Mr Mole Gets Lost 272
Mr Squirrel Won't
 Sleep 166
My Father he Died 125
My Funny Family 223
My Grandmother
 Sent Me 301
My Hands 221
My Hobby Horse 348
My Mummy's Maid 317
My Shadow 380
Naughty Bears, The 12
Naughty Broom,
 The 214
Naughty Chester
 Chick 38
New Cat, The 218
Night Sounds 380
Night-night Bear 382
No One Like You 298
North Wind Doth
 Blow, The 156
Not Another Bear 276
Oats and Beans 204
Ode to Ghosts 95
Oh Dear, What Can
 the Matter Be? 172
Old Bandy Legs 317
Old Everest 202
Old Joe Brown 268
Old John
 Muddlecombe 268
Old King Cole 332
Old Roger is Dead 44
On Oath 37
Once I Saw a Little
 Bird 156
One Bad Bunny 212

One Dark Night 68
One Finger, One
 Thumb 28
One Hen Pecking 285
One Little Indian 317
One Stormy Night 228
One, Two 317
One, Two, Buckle
 My Shoe 61
One, Two, Three,
 Four, Five 60
Oscar the Octopus 271
Over the Hills and
 Far Away 45
Oxen, The 178
Parliament Soldiers 36
Pease Pudding Hot 204
Perfect Puppy, A 244
Peter Meets a
 Dragon 302
Peter Piper 301
Peter, Peter, Pumpkin
 Eater 370
Pigs will be Pigs 198
Pit, Pat 365
Polly Piglet's
 Surprise Party 346
Poor Old Robinson
 Crusoe! 268
Pop Goes the Weasel
 204
Priest, The 365
Punctuality 37
Punctuate 364
Queen of Hearts,
 The 333
Rain 348
Rain 364
Rain, Rain, Go
 Away 28
Rat, A 37
Red Sky 348
Richard Dick 37
Ride Away 36
Robert Rowley 301
Robin and Richard 189
Robin and the Wren,
 The 36
Robin Hood 348
Robin the Bobbin 205

Round About 10
Round About There 140
Round and Round
 the Garden 18
Row, Row, Row Your
 Boat 221
Rub-a-dub Dub 269
Rumpelstiltskin 350
Sad Clown, The 320
Sailor Went to
 Sea, A 45
Scary Adventure, A 288
Scrub Your Dirty
 Face 28
See-saw, Sacradown 44
Shoes 141
Shrovetide 365
Simple Simon 370
Sing a Song of
 Sixpence 205
Sippity, Sippity
 Sup 316
Smart Bear and
 the Foolish Bear,
 The 196
Smelly Pup 56
Smiley Crocodile,
 The 122
Sneeze on Monday 29
Sniffle 306
Snowy and Blowy 262
Solomon Grundy 269
Sparky the Baby
 Dragon 362
Spellbound 381
Spelling Lesson, A 58
Spin Dame 36
Spooks' Ball, The 138
Squeaky Van, The 374
Squirrel, The 11
Staying at Grandma's
 70
Sunshine 317
Swan Swam Over
 the Sea 300
Tabby Cat and the
 Cockerel 336
Take the Ghost
 Train 94
Tall Shop 141

Teddy Bear, Teddy
 Bear 18
Ten Little Fingers 221
Ten Little Men 333
Ten o' Clock Scholar 10
There was a Crooked
 Man 124
There Was a King
 and he had Three
 Daughters 333
There Was a Little
 Boy 370
There Was a Little
 Boy and a
 Little Girl 349
There Was a Man,
 and His Name
 Was Dob 300
There Was a Piper 77
There Was an Old
 Man With a Beard 252
There's No Room
 Here 30
This Little Piggy 108
Three Jovial
 Welshmen, The 60
Three Wise Men of
 Gotham 125
Three Young Rats 61
Tiger Tales 310
Tiger Tricks 106
To Market, To
 Market 108
To Market, to
 Market, to Buy
 a Fat Pig 108
To the Magpie 10
Tom he Was a
 Piper's Son 11
Tom, Tom, the
 Piper's Son 189
Tommy Snooks and
 Bessy Brooks 371
Tommy Thumb 269
Tommy Trot 141
Tommy's Shop 364
Tractor Trouble 192
Tumbling 109
Tweedle-dum and
 Tweedle-dee 76

Two Fat Gentlemen 109
Two Little Dicky
 Birds 157
Two Little Men in a
 Flying Saucer 108
Warning 349
Wash, Hands, Wash 220
Washing Up 348
Watch Out! 237
Way Down Yonder
 in the Maple
 Swamp 44
We're All in the
 Dumps 76
Wee Willie Winkie 370
Whale of a Time, A 181
What is the Rhyme
 for Porringer? 332
What's the News? 348
Wheels on the Bus,
 The 18
When Famed King
 Arthur Ruled
 This Land 333
When Jacky's a
 Very Good Boy 371
Where Am I? 316
Where Are You? 236
Where Go the Boats? 178
Where's Wanda? 292
While We Were
 Walking 157
Who Can Save the
 Chicks? 126
Willie Wastle 36
Wind, The 381
Wine and Cakes 364
Witch's Brew 59
Without a Growl 237
Wonky Bear 32
Woolly Coats 284
Yankee Doodle 93
Yellow Digger, The 240
Yes You Can! 277
You Can Do It,
 Dilly Duck! 308
You Need a Cow! 284
Young Roger Came
 Tapping 188